Windows

Mary Campbell

Osborne **McGraw-Hill**
2600 Tenth Street
Berkeley, California 94710
U.S.A.

For information on software, translations, or book distributors outside of the
U.S.A., please write to Osborne **McGraw-Hill** at the above address.

Simply Windows

1234567890 DOC 998765432

ISBN 0-07-881743-9

Acknowledgments

I would like to thank the many individuals who gave so much of their time and talent to help shape this book:

Gabrielle Lawrence for her work on all aspects of the project.

Kenna Wood and Allen Wyatt for their idea to do this *Simply...* series. Their perceptive look at the marketplace allowed them to realize that many users need a quick way to get at the essentials of a software package, with only a minimal time investment.

Frances Stack for reading the manuscript and helping to fine-tune its contents for our audience.

Jill Pisoni for double-checking the chapters as they came in, making sure every chapter was complete.

Carol Henry for her copyedit, helping this to be a book that makes learning Windows easy for anyone.

Susie Kim for her wonderful rendering of the artwork ideas. Susie's work makes this an inviting book that clearly illustrates Windows' main features.

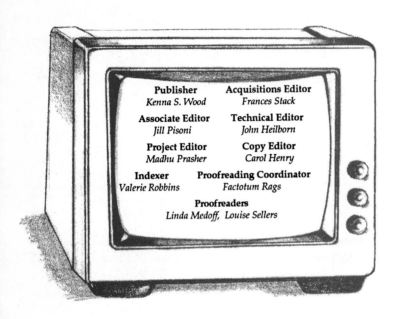

Publisher
Kenna S. Wood

Acquisitions Editor
Frances Stack

Associate Editor
Jill Pisoni

Technical Editor
John Heilborn

Project Editor
Madhu Prasher

Copy Editor
Carol Henry

Indexer
Valerie Robbins

Proofreading Coordinator
Factotum Rags

Proofreaders
Linda Medoff, Louise Sellers

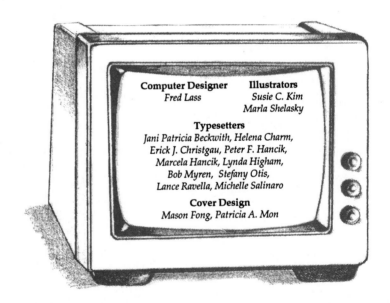

Computer Designer
Fred Lass

Illustrators
Susie C. Kim
Marla Shelasky

Typesetters
Jani Patricia Beckwith, Helena Charm,
Erick J. Christgau, Peter F. Hancik,
Marcela Hancik, Lynda Higham,
Bob Myren, Stefany Otis,
Lance Ravella, Michelle Salinaro

Cover Design
Mason Fong, Patricia A. Mon

Contents

It's Simple to Use This Lay-Flat Binding ...

Open this book to any page you choose and crease back the left-hand page by pressing along the length of the spine with your fingers. Now, the book will stay open until you're ready to go on to another page.

Unlike regular book bindings, this special binding won't weaken or crack when you crease back the pages. It's tough, durable, and resilient—designed to withstand years of daily use. So go ahead, put this book to the test and use it as often as you like.

What Windows Has to Offer

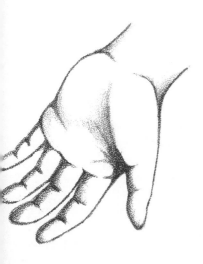

Windows is a program that makes it easier to use your computer's features and the software you purchase. Windows also gives your computer new capabilities, such as running several of your applications at the same time.

Before Windows came along, you had to use the keyboard or the mouse to define each request you made to your computer. The rules for entering your requests were not intuitive, and it was easy to make a mistake in typing your entries. If you are like many users, at times you may have been frustrated by the complexity of trying to get things done. With Windows, you can accomplish tasks with a minimum of typing.

Windows presents the information you work with and the tools for performing your tasks in a *graphical* way. Windows presents a full screen of this graphical information allowing you to view and make many options on one screen. Rather than having to remember a complex sequence of entries to communicate with your computer and its software, Windows lets you select pictures of tasks and data, called *icons*.

Windows offers other advantages. For example, you can use Windows to manage the information stored in your computer. You can start and run multiple programs at the same time, in their own *windows*. Each window can contain different information. Windows even provides *accessory* programs, such as a calendar and a calculator to help you with your business tasks.

In this chapter you will have an opportunity to take a quick look at the way some of the Windows features and accessories can help you get your job done every day.

Using the Graphical User Interface

Although working with your computer will always require some typing, Windows's *graphical user interface* lets you perform most of your tasks by selecting a picture of what you want. These pictures of tasks and information are called *icons*.

You have seen icons on many familiar objects—on the dashboard of your car, for instance, where the oil light might display an oil can or the headlight switch might show a representation of a headlight. Other icons you may have seen are a picture of an airplane on a road sign directing you to an airport; or the green silhouette of a person walking on a pedestrian crossing signal. These symbols are instantly recognizable; you don't need to read anything to see what they mean. With Windows, the screen icon serves the same purpose—to show you what task the icon performs. There is no chance for making a typing mistake, because no typing is required for the selection.

GUI stands for Graphical User Interface. GUI (pronounced "gooey") is the latest trend (and the latest buzzword) in computers. Windows's GUI means that you can handle much of your interaction with the computer through graphics, rather than typing.

The Need for a New Way of Working

Because Windows uses icons to represent information and tasks, you will need a device that can move from icon to icon and make quick selections. Although the keyboard can be used for this purpose, it is not the best tool because of the number of keystrokes required for moving from object to object and making selections.

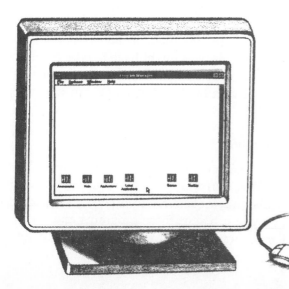

A *mouse* device offers many advantages over the keyboard; to move from place to place on your computer screen, all you have to do is roll the mouse across the top of your desk. The current position on your screen is marked by a *mouse pointer*. Your hand movements as you roll the mouse control the amount and direction of the pointer movement. This pointer often looks like an arrow, but it changes shape depending on its location and the task you are performing. Once you have positioned the mouse pointer, you can then select the desired object by pressing a button on the top of the mouse. You will learn all about the various mouse actions in Chapter 2.

Using Programs with Windows

Programs are a set of instructions that direct your computer to store a memo that you type, or compute a budget, or draw a graph. Many programs are designed specifically to run under Windows, so they can take advantage of Windows's ability to run several programs concurrently. These programs also make the best use of the graphical features that Windows offers.

Windows can also run most programs written for DOS. DOS is an operating system that was designed to manage the resources of a computer system. Although DOS is required to run Windows, DOS provides only a few of Windows's features, and does not offer the important graphical interface advantages of Windows. There are some programs designed specifically for DOS, and which do not use the more advanced features of Windows. If you use these programs, you might have to type all of your selections. Also, these programs were designed to be "stand-alone" (the only application program running within the computer at any one time).

About the Program Manager

Windows provides a Program Manager to manage your programs. Collectively, all of the programs that perform tasks for you, such as word processing or financial calculations, are referred to as *application programs*. With the Program Manager you can start these programs and organize them into groups of similar programs. The Program Manager window is the window that appears when you first start Windows (unless you have changed the standard Windows settings).

The Program Manager window displays program group icons representing a set of one or more programs that you can run. Normally you will have a program group icon for each general category of software that you use. For example, the icons for the Windows accessory programs, which are available from any program or task, are accessed from the Program Manager window. The Accessories perform tasks and provide tools that you might want to use at any time during a Windows session, such as providing the correct time, a calendar, or a notepad, or performing mathematical calculations. When you activate the Accessories group icon, the individual Accessories icons are displayed in place of the program group icon.

The icons in Program Manager are either unique icons for a specific program, like this one:

Paintbrush

or a group icon, which is the same for any program group, and looks like this:

Non-Windows Applications

The most common way to start an application is through the Program Manager. In Chapter 7, you will learn how to open a program group and then select the program that you want to run.

Using Multiple Windows

Unless you are neater than most people, your desk at the office probably has more than one project on it. This may be to remind you to begin work on a new task, or because you're working on more than one thing at a time; or maybe you need to look up information from one project and use it in another.

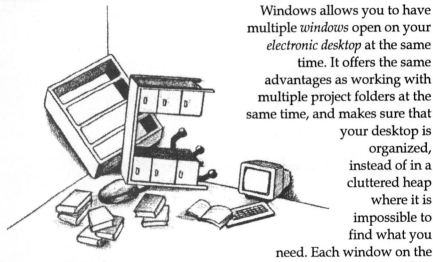

Windows allows you to have multiple *windows* open on your *electronic desktop* at the same time. It offers the same advantages as working with multiple project folders at the same time, and makes sure that your desktop is organized, instead of in a cluttered heap where it is impossible to find what you need. Each window on the desktop is a rectangular workspace that you can use for displaying data or other information.

Another advantage of using multiple windows is that you have a broader perspective of what you are doing with your computer at any one time. The windows can be resized and repositioned to allow you to look at several tasks at once. This wider view is like being able to look into the windows of a toy store, a furniture store, and a clothing outlet at the same time. Since your view

includes all three shops, you can consider Christmas gift ideas for several people, as well as explore the latest fashion trends. You can also decide when you're ready to purchase a new toy and then focus on the toy store display when the time is right.

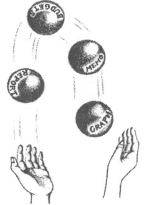

The Windows desktop is flexible: You can stack the open windows atop one another and view one at a time. This lets you concentrate on all the details of the information in a particular window. You can also switch to a different desktop *layout* that shows all the open windows at one time. Windows makes it easier for you to juggle several tasks at the same time, easily moving from one to the other; you can even transfer information between applications.

Handling File Management Tasks

The *files* in your computer are organized collections of information. Files, too, are represented in Windows by icons on your screen and can be selected with ease. All of the tasks that you want to accomplish with files are available in a File Manager menu that shows the different options and makes it easy to select the operation that you want.

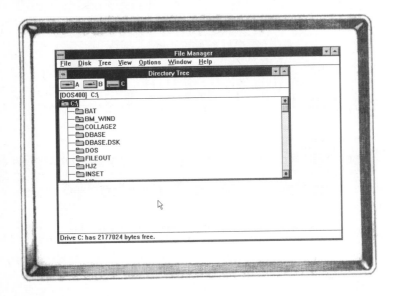

The Windows File Manager makes it easy to view, access, and manipulate the files stored on a disk. It clearly displays the structure of your disks; you can get an overview look that shows how your disks are organized, or a detailed look at each file on the disk, depending on what you need to accomplish.

In addition to working with files in the File Manager, you can use File Manager to start programs. The details of using File Manager are presented in Chapter 8.

Using Accessories

Even if your office is sparsely furnished, you probably have a number of basic tools to help you get your job done efficiently, such as a calculator, a notebook, and a telephone. Windows provides some accessories that make working with the computer easier. Just as you can use your office accessories at any time, the Windows accessories are available regardless of what other tasks you are working on. Having your tools available to you at any time is an important advantage. At times you will even be able to use a Windows accessory instead of another program that provides the same features, because the accessory is more readily available.

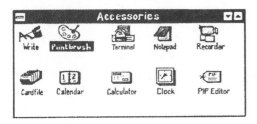

Windows provides even more accessories than you will find in the average office—ten accessory features are available through the Accessories window, and another feature called Clipboard is available through any Windows application. You will probably use some of these on a regular basis, and others only occasionally, depending on the work you do.

In Chapters 11 and 12 you will have an opportunity to take a closer look at some of the accessories. For now, let's take a quick look at some of the tasks that the Windows accessories perform, to get a clearer idea of how they can help you in particular.

- The Write accessory lets you type documents and store them on disk. If you have ever used a word processing program for creating memos or reports, you will find that Write performs essentially the same tasks.

- The Notepad is used for storing brief notes or even short documents. It is just like a small notepad that you might keep next to the phone or in your pocket. You might want to activate the Notepad window when you need to record information from a phone call while you are working in another Windows application. After jotting down the note, you can return to the other application window and finish your work, and then follow up on the note when you have time.

- If you have ever used index cards to record bibliographic entries, vendor information, or warranties on purchased items, you will feel instantly at home with the Cardfile accessory.

- The helpful Clipboard feature is much like a real clipboard that you might carry with you from meeting to meeting to write down important facts. You can then share what you learned at one meeting with individuals at the next meeting as you review your Clipboard notes. The Windows Clipboard is available through any Windows application; using Clipboard, you can cut and paste information from one window to another, and bring information from many different applications together in one summary report.

- The Clock, Calendar, and Calculator perform the tasks implied by their names. You can access them quickly to check the date or time, review your next week's appointments, or compute an invoice entry.

- The Paintbrush accessory lets you create and change graphic images. You can use the Paintbrush in black and white, or with a full palette of colors.

- The Terminal accessory lets you exchange information with another computer.

- With the Recorder, you can record the keystrokes that perform a task so you can perform the same task again later by just pressing one key.

- The PIF Editor lets you change the settings that DOS programs use when you run them in Windows.

Keys to Success

The advantages that Windows offers are these:

- An environment that makes it easy to work, with many helpful tools

- A graphical user interface that saves keystrokes and typing errors

- The ability to arrange information on your screen in multiple windows, so you can see exactly what you need to finish a project quickly

- The ability to run several programs at once, so you don't have to waste time saving your work, exiting a program, and starting another

- File management tools that require a minimum of typing and show a clear visual file structure

- A collection of accessories that make it easier to perform your job

What Do They Mean By...?

Access   The ability to use programs and data.

Application   A program or series of programs that allow your computer to perform a set of tasks.

Desktop   The arrangement of information on your computer screen that simulates the information you might have on the top of your office desk. This visual electronic desktop shows files, programs, and other computer tasks as objects that you can use and control.

File   An organized collection of information on a disk.

Graphical User Interface   An interface that minimizes the typing you must do to accomplish tasks. You can select an icon that represents a task or information, instead of having to type commands.

Icon   A pictorial representation of a task or information.

Insertion Point   A symbol that marks your current screen location during keyboard entries.

Layout   The arrangement of text and other information on the desktop.

Mouse   A hand-held device that you roll across your desktop. The mouse movements are converted into corresponding changes in the location of a pointer in the workspace. Buttons on top of the mouse let you make selections of objects on the screen once you have positioned the pointer.

Pointer   A special symbol on the screen used to mark your current location as you move the mouse.

Program   A set of instructions that allows your computer to perform tasks. Also called an application.

Window   A rectangular workspace on the desktop that displays information or performs a task.

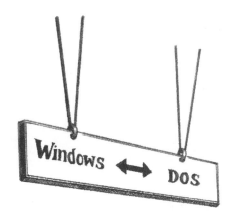

Starting Windows 2

DOS is the *operating system* that controls the resources of your computer and the programs you use in it. An operating system is itself a program, designed to manage your computer's components and insure that they work together properly. This means DOS must manage the memory of your machine, where active programs and information are stored on a temporary basis, as well as the permanent storage of information on your hard disk. DOS also manages the display of information on your screen or printer. Before you can place any other program into the memory of your computer, DOS must be there first.

Since Windows is a program that supplements DOS's features, Windows, too, requires DOS to be loaded and functioning in your system. You will find that the steps for starting DOS and then Windows are easy to remember. And once Windows is active, its graphical user interface makes learning Windows tasks fun and easy to do.

Starting DOS

Starting DOS in your computer is as simple as turning it on. Since Windows can only work on a computer with a hard disk, you must have a hard disk if you plan to use Windows. All of the DOS information needed for startup will be stored on the hard disk. If you have other disk drives that accept removable disks (such as floppy disks), you will want to insure that these drives are empty during the startup process. A data disk left in the floppy drive will result in a failed attempt to start DOS and an error message displayed on your system.

Successfully starting DOS on your system is called *booting* the system. It results in the display of a DOS *prompt* on your screen. The C:\> prompt tells you that drive C is the *active* drive, and DOS is ready to respond to your next request. The active drive is the one DOS will access to look for your information, unless you direct it to look elsewhere.

Your next request will usually be to start up an application, such as 1-2-3, Windows, or WordPerfect, or a DOS command for a task such as copying a file.

Starting Windows

You can start any DOS program by simply typing the name of the program, which is also the name of the file that contains the instructions for the program. Program filenames have an extension that follows the main filename; this extension is usually .COM or .EXE. The Windows 3.0 program file is called WIN.EXE and is started by typing **WIN**.

The location on the hard disk that contains a program is called the *directory*. Think of a directory location as a position on a tree structure that branches out from the *root* or *main directory* on the disk. You can have as many as eight directory levels, although you'll probably find that three or four levels can handle the file needs of the average system. A representation of the directory structure for your drive C might look something like this directory tree.

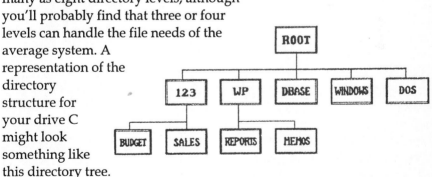

In some cases you must activate the directory that contains a program. However, if you installed Windows in a conventional manner (as described in Appendix A, "Installing Windows"), this extra step of changing the Windows directory is unnecessary. Using the procedure in Appendix A, you added the directions for locating Windows to a PATH statement that takes effect when you start DOS. Regardless of the directory from which you start DOS, it can find Windows because the PATH statement tells DOS where to look.

Thus you can start Windows from any location on the hard disk, by simply typing the name of the Windows program, as follows:

- Type **WIN**.
- Press ENTER.

DOS searches for the WIN program on your hard disk and displays the initial Windows screen:

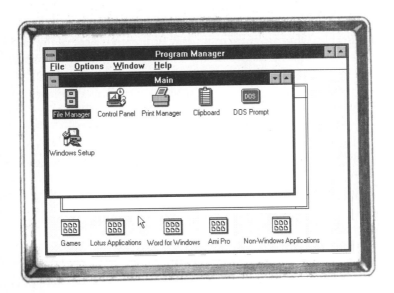

Starting Windows

Start DOS by turning on your computer. You must make the Windows program active in the RAM memory of your system before you can use its features. Since Windows requires the DOS operating system, you will need to make DOS active first. To start Windows, start DOS, and type **WIN** and press ENTER.

Understanding the Windows Desktop

Your desktop in the office contains active projects, documents that you received in today's mail, and accessories such as a calendar and a calculator to help you get your job done. The Windows desktop offers an electronic version of the same things.

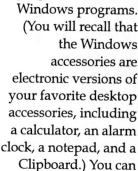

The Windows electronic desktop is where you will work with Windows accessories, application programs, and other Windows programs. (You will recall that the Windows accessories are electronic versions of your favorite desktop accessories, including a calculator, an alarm clock, a notepad, and a Clipboard.) You can have a window open on the desktop for each program that is running. Windows gives you the capability to manage the tasks in each of these windows.

If you installed Windows with the directions in Appendix A, your initial screen (shown previously) displays the Windows Program Manager. (You can read the words Program Manager in the title bar at the top of the window.) The Program Manager is one of a number of programs that you get when you purchase Windows. It is one of two programs that Windows uses to start other programs. In Chapter 7 you will learn all the details of how the Program Manager works, but for now, let's use your Program Manager window to explore the various components of the Windows desktop.

When you start Windows, your display will show a Program Manager window similar to the one illustrated here, with icons in the workspace.

Some of these icons may have been expanded to other windows that partially obscure the Program Manager workspace.

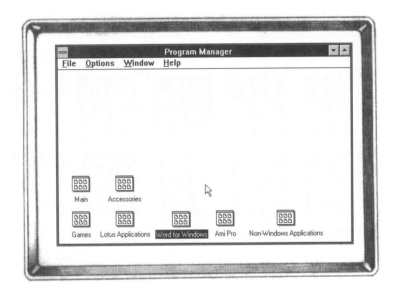

If your screen does not display the Program Manager when you first start Windows, it means that your copy of Windows has been customized to display other information. If this is the case, you'll need to use the Windows Task List to get to the Program Manager. The Task List is a list of all the windows that you can activate. Follow this procedure:

- If you're using a mouse, click any Control Menu box. Choose Switch To, and the Task List appears. Then move the pointer to Program Manager and *double-click* the left mouse button.

- If you're using a keyboard, press CTRL-ESC (the connecting hyphen means press both the CTRL and ESC keys at the same time). This displays the Task List. Use the arrow keys on your keyboard to highlight Program Manager in the Task List, and press ENTER.

Note: Double-clicking means pressing the left mouse button twice in rapid succession. (See "Using a Mouse with Windows" later in this chapter.)

Changing the Current Task

If you have more than one active task, you can use the Task List to make another task the current task. Press CTRL-ESC to activate the Task List. Highlight the task you want to work with. Press ENTER to finalize your selection.

What Is a Window?

A *window* is a rectangle on your Windows desktop that is used to display an application or a document. Regardless of what type of information is in a window, each window has some standard components. Like the windows in buildings, the various parts of electronic windows can be named and identified.

The various windows also have special components, based on the tasks for which you use the window. For example, a document

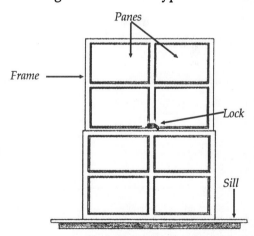

window sometimes has a scroll bar on the right side that you can use to move quickly from the beginning to the end of the document. Another scroll bar is also found at the bottom of a document window, so you can move from side to side within a wide document. In addition, the programs will often have additional components. For example, an accessory window that is used for painting on the screen contains a color palette and numerous drawing tools that are not needed when you are working in a document to create a memo.

The Window Components

Let's take a look at the various components of a window—although you do not need to memorize the name of each window component, you will want to closely examine all of them. The terms introduced here are part of the basic language of the Windows environment. As you work through this book, you will have an opportunity to learn and work with this

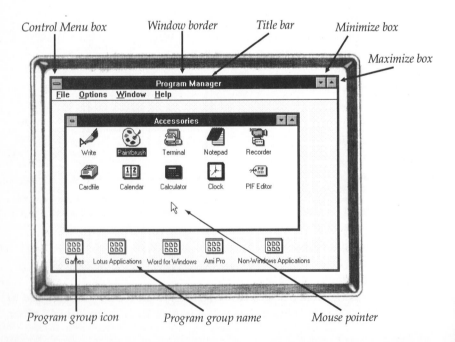

language. Since all of your programs will now run under Windows, understanding basic Windows terms is the starting point for learning more about individual Windows tasks. Trying to learn Windows without this vocabulary of special terms would be like living in a foreign country without knowing at least a few words of the native language.

The top line of the Program Manager window is divided into four small rectangular areas:

Control Menu box   *Title bar*   *Minimize box*

Maximize box

- The small square on the left is called the Control Menu box. It provides access to options for sizing and moving the window.

- The main area in the center of the line is called the *title bar*. In this window, Program Manager is the title of the window.

- The *Minimize box* at the right end of the line is used to minimize (close) the window and display it as an icon.

- The *Maximize/Restore box* is at the far right end of the line. This box is a Maximize box when it contains a single arrow that points upward; in this state it is used to make the window the size of the screen. The box is called the Restore box when it contains arrows that point both up and down; in this state it can make a window larger or smaller, and is used to restore a window to its previous size. You can always distinguish a Maximize box from a Restore box by looking at the arrows; an up arrow only is Maximize, and an up-and-down arrow is Restore.

Just under the title bar line is the *menu bar*, which displays the main menu options available in a window.

Beneath the menu bar is the *workspace*—usually the largest area of the window. This is where you will work on Windows tasks.

All windows have *borders*. Window borders are the edges of the window and are used for changing its size.

Some windows contain an optional *status bar* at the bottom, used for the display of messages. You will see many windows without a status bar.

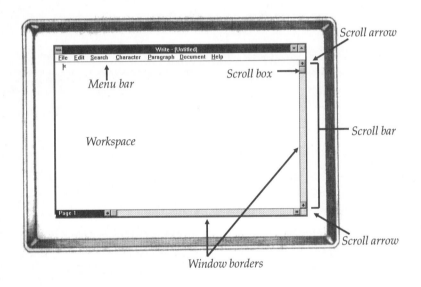

Document windows have a *vertical scroll bar* on the right side and a *horizontal scroll bar* at the bottom of the workspace, to allow you to scroll up and down or left and right to see information that is not currently displayed in the window. A *scroll box* is a small square positioned within a scroll bar, which indicates how close you are to the top or bottom (or left or right edge) of the information in the workspace. You can slide the scroll box to move through information in a window. *Scroll arrows* appear at either end of a scroll bar. You will learn how to use scroll arrows to move slowly through the information in the window.

The Icons on Your Initial Windows Screen

As mentioned in Chapter 1, icons are graphic representations of data and tasks. Icons are important visual elements in Windows's graphical user interface. You can move your mouse pointer to an icon and *select* it to start a program and perform many other actions.

The icons that are displayed in the Program Manager window represent groups of programs that you can access from the Program Manager. The program groups that you are likely to see are

- Games

- Accessories

- Main

- Windows Applications

- Non-Windows Applications

Try selecting each icon to see what programs each group icon contains.

Using a Mouse with Windows

If you have a mouse, you can use it to reduce the amount of typing that you need to do to complete tasks. Windows's many icons are specifically designed for mouse selections.

There are several types of mouse devices. Some can be rolled across your desk to change the location of the mouse pointer on your screen. Others have a *trackball* that you roll with your hand. Once you have the mouse pointer positioned where you want it, you can click the mouse button(s) to make your selections. If you have enjoyed video games, using a mouse will come very naturally to you, because you have probably developed excellent eye/hand coordination as you have mastered the games. If you have been using a keyboard for years, you will need to be patient for a few weeks and allow yourself to adjust to the benefits that using a mouse can offer.

The mouse pointer on your screen will change as you move the mouse around to different areas of a window and perform various Windows operations. Most of the time the pointer appears as an arrow, but don't be surprised, as you learn new tasks, when it changes shape.

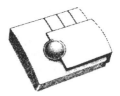

Your mouse may have one, two, or three buttons on top. If your mouse has multiple buttons, you will want to use the left one. No matter how many buttons are on your mouse, you can perform only three actions with a mouse.

Mouse Actions

Clicking the mouse button means pressing it once and releasing it.

Note: Normally you will want to position the mouse pointer on an object in a window before you click the mouse button, since clicking an object means you select it (to be the result of a Windows operation). Clicking and other mouse actions have no effect unless you are pointing at an object.

Double-clicking means pressing the left mouse button twice in rapid succession after pointing to the desired object. Double-clicking is used to start programs, for example.

A third mouse action is called *dragging*. After pointing to the desired object, you press the left mouse button and hold it down while moving the mouse across your desk. You will learn how dragging is used to relocate or resize a window, to select several files that are adjacent to one another in a list, and to select text.

Using the Keyboard

Even with the advantages of a mouse in Windows, you cannot completely eliminate the use of your computer's keyboard. You will need the keyboard for typing information, and there will be times when you will prefer to use the keyboard to make selections.

To select an icon with the keyboard, you must first highlight it. If it is in the current window, you can use the keyboard arrow keys to highlight it, and then press ENTER to select it. To move to an icon representing another program group or window, press CTRL-F6 or CTRL-TAB.

Sometimes the keyboard alternative requires about the same amount of time as using the mouse. At other times one method may seem to be much quicker than the other. Choose whatever method is best for you—the results will be the same. You may feel there is more to remember when using the keyboard; this is because there are many unique key-combinations for performing Windows tasks. Sometimes you will want to mix and match your keyboard and mouse actions to accomplish different tasks. A number of keyboard shortcuts are available in Windows that might be more economical for you than making selections with your mouse. These keyboard shortcuts will be noted throughout the chapters.

Ending a Windows Session

To end your current
Windows session,
you need to close any
open Windows and
exit the Windows
program. Just as you
would close all the
windows in your
house before a long
trip to keep out rain
or intruders, you will
want to close the
windows on your

screen to protect their contents before you exit Windows. To close a
window, double-click the Control Menu box of the application or document.

*Warning: Turning your machine off without first closing the open win-
dows and exiting Windows properly can result in a loss of your data.*

If you have a number of windows open, instead of closing the windows
one by one you can make a single close request from the Program Manager
Control Menu. To do this, move the mouse pointer over the Program
Manager Control Menu box, and click the left mouse button. Choose Close
from the Control Menu by moving the mouse pointer to Close and clicking
it. You can also choose Exit from the File menu to end your Windows
session.

To confirm that
you want to end
the session,
Windows displays
a dialog box that
looks like this:

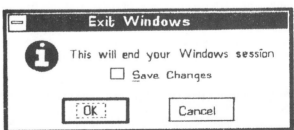

If you want to save the changes made to the size and position of the group windows in the Program Manager during the current Windows session, select the check box next to Save Changes. An *X* appears in the check box to indicate the option is selected. If the box is not marked, changes will not be saved when you exit.

The two options at the bottom of the dialog box are called *command buttons*. Clicking the OK button confirms that you want to exit Windows. Clicking the Cancel button tells Windows to ignore your initial request to end the Windows session.

Tip: As a shortcut to closing Windows, you can also double-click the Program Manager Control Menu box, or press ALT-F4.

Ending a Windows Session

When you end a Windows session, you close all open windows, remove the Windows program from memory, and return to the DOS prompt. The quickest way to end a session is to double-click the Program Manager Control Menu box, or press ALT-F4.

Keys to Success

In this chapter you have learned about the following basic Windows features and options:

- To start Windows, you must first start the DOS operating system in your computer. Make sure drive A is empty, and turn your system on; then start Windows by typing **WIN**.

- Windows is designed to work best with a mouse. There are three mouse actions: click, double-click, and drag.

- The Program Manager is an important Windows program that can start your programs and perform many other tasks.

- A quick way to close Windows is to double-click the Program Manager Control Menu box. When you end a Windows session, you return to DOS.

What Do They Mean By...?

Active   A program that is running is considered active. Menu items that are active are available for selection.

Booting   Starting your computer and loading the operating system software into memory.

Clicking   Pressing and releasing the mouse button.

Command Button   A selectable button on the screen that begins an action.

Directory   A list of related files on a disk.

Double-clicking   Pressing the mouse button twice in rapid succession.

Dragging   Pressing the mouse button, holding it down, and moving the mouse (or the ball on a trackball) to make a selection or perform a task.

Operating System   A program that manages the resources of your computer system and the programs that you use in it.

Prompt   A message displayed by Windows requesting a response, or the DOS prompt that appears when you exit Windows.

RAM   A temporary storage area within your computer where active programs and temporary copies of current data are stored.

Select   To choose an item on the screen.

Selected   A selected item is one that is chosen; it appears highlighted or flashing on the screen.

Working with Menus and Dialog Boxes

Windows uses *menus* to present your options and selections, just as restaurants do when you eat out. Most restaurants have special menus for different times of the day to present popular choices for the meal typically eaten at that time. These special menus make it easier for you to focus on the choices that are available at the time you're there. Within each menu you find separate sections for beverages, side dishes, entrees, and desserts. These sections organize the various options in each category that are available.

Windows's menus, too, present its features in an easy-to-select format. Each menu provides a set of related choices for files, windows, on-screen help information, and other options. This organization makes it easy to know which menu to open so you can accomplish a specific task. In each Windows menu there are sections that organize groups of selections into related choices.

After you make your menu selections, Windows either begins your task or displays a *dialog box*. Dialog boxes let you communicate with Windows about what you want to do; they contain a selection of information with which you define and refine the task that Windows is performing for you. You'll want to learn thoroughly how to access all the options in the menus and dialog boxes. By combining these techniques with what you've already learned about selecting items on the Windows desktop, you'll be able to tell Windows exactly what to do.

Working with Menus

The Windows menu choices are always in the menu bar at the top of the Program Manager window, ready for you to select the one you want. You can use either the mouse or the keyboard to select any of the four menus: File, Options, Windows, and Help. Selecting one of these options displays, or "pulls down" a list of options for that menu. This *pull-down* menu lets you see the full range of choices and make a selection. You can use either the mouse or the keyboard to make your selections within a menu. Some menu options also have *quick-keys*, which are special key-combinations you can press to make a request more quickly, without having to select from the menu. The next time you want to use one of these options, just press the quick-key combination and you will not need to pull down the menu.

In addition to the menu options provided by the menu bar, you can also use the Windows Control Menu to work with the Program Manager window. Although you will activate the Control Menu in a different manner, its pull-down menu and the selections that you make from it follow the same procedures you will learn for the menu bar options.

Selecting from a Menu

You can select a menu and view its pull-down options with either a mouse or the keyboard. These techniques work for Windows menus as well as the menus within any Windows-compatible applications program.

To activate a pull-down menu with the mouse:

- Click one of the options in the menu bar.

To activate a pull-down menu from the keyboard:

- Press ALT. This activates the menu bar and displays a highlight on the File menu option. The highlight means the File menu option is selected.

- Then use the keyboard arrow keys to highlight the desired menu bar option; press ENTER to see the pull-down menu.

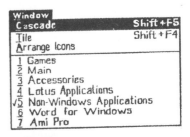

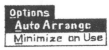

Another keyboard method for activating a pull-down menu is to type the underlined letter in the desired option. For example, type **F** to select File, or **O** to select Options. If you use this technique, you can type a *combination keystroke* rather than two sequential keystrokes; that is, you can press ALT and F simultaneously (ALT-F) to select the File pull-down menu.

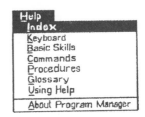

Selecting an Option on a Menu

One way to tell Windows what you want to do is to make a selection from a menu. To activate a menu and make a selection, follow these steps:

1. Click the desired option in the menu bar, or press ALT and type the underlined letter in the menu name.

2. When the pull-down menu appears, click the desired option, or type the underlined letter in the option, or highlight the desired option and press ENTER.

About the Pull-Down Menus

The pull-down menus that appear when you select an option from the menu bar have some consistent elements, regardless of the menu that you select. The options in some of these pull-down menus are divided by lines into related groups. The only significance of these lines is to make it easier for you to find the command you want. The File pull-down menu, for instance, has a section for commands that affect a program group, a section for the Run command used to start programs, and a section for the command used to exit Windows.

Notice that some menu options have an ellipsis (...) after their names. An ellipsis indicates that more information is required to process the selection. When you select one of these options, you'll see a *dialog box* that presents all the settings or choices you need to make, in one organized location.

Some menu options may appear dimmed—displayed lighter than the other choices in the menu. When dimmed, these menu options are not available for your selection.

About the Quick-Keys

Some menu options present a quick-key shortcut option listed to their right on the menu. These *shortcut keys* can be used to invoke the menu selection directly, without going through another menu or dialog box.

Look at the File pull-down menu, for example; you can see that the quick-key for Open is ENTER, and for Delete, it is DEL. This means you can open a program group by selecting its icon and pressing ENTER, rather than pulling down the File menu and choosing Open. The shortcut for deleting a program or program group is to select its icon and press DEL, rather than pulling down the File menu

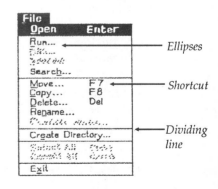

and choosing Delete. All you need is the quick-key to perform the action. Over time you will begin to remember these shortcuts because you will see them so frequently in the pull-down menus. Begin now to use them as often as you like if you feel they save you time and keystrokes.

Selecting Options from the Pull-Down Menus

To select an option from one of the pull-down menus, you can click it with a mouse. Or, to use the keyboard, type the underlined letter in the option, or use the arrow keys to highlight your option and then press ENTER. If the option has no further dialog boxes (there is no ellipsis next to it), Windows begins to execute the selected task. Otherwise, you will see the next dialog box where you need to make the additional choices.

Activating the Control Menu

The Program Manager provides another menu that is not available from the menu bar. This menu is called the Control Menu, and you access it from the Control Menu box in the upper-left corner of the window.

Both types of windows—application and document—have a Control Menu box. (You'll learn more about these windows in Chapter 4.) From both window types you can access the Control Menu by clicking this box with the mouse. In application windows you can also press ALT-SPACEBAR to access the Control Menu. (You can tell you are in an application window by looking at the name of the application in the title bar. Also, the horizontal bar and the Control Menu box are larger in an application window than in a document window.) In document windows you can also press ALT-HYPHEN to open the Control Menu. (This is the window without a menu bar.)

The pull-down Control Menu provides options for sizing and moving the window, switching to other windows, and closing the window. The organization of the Control Menu and methods for selecting its options are the same as for the pull-down menus that are attached to the menu bar.

Canceling a Selection

If you inadvertently display a menu that you do not want, you can put the menu away without selecting anything from it. To do this with a mouse, just click anywhere in the Program Manager workspace to put away the menu. On the keyboard, you can press ESC or ALT. Either way, the menu is no longer active and you can proceed with another request.

Tip: You might need to use this technique if you forget to select an icon before proceeding with your menu selection. After canceling the menu selection, you can choose the correct icon.

If you pull down the wrong menu, you do not have to cancel it to access the one that you want. Instead, press the RIGHT ARROW or LEFT ARROW key to pull down the menu on either side of the menu that is showing, or just click another menu bar option.

Canceling a Menu Selection

If you pull down the wrong menu, you can always cancel your request by pressing ESC, or ALT, or clicking another menu or location.

Working with Dialog Boxes

Dialog boxes are a significant component of the Windows interface—they allow you to refine the information you present to the program, so that it executes your request exactly as you intend. Dialog boxes initially display the current *default settings*. These are the options you get if you do not make a change to the settings. If you like the default settings, all you need to do is to tell Windows to proceed. At other times you will want to change as many of the options as you need to get exactly the results you want.

Dialog boxes are a lot like government survey forms, or the tickets that food servers in a diner use to take a customer's order. All of the options are listed in one place to allow quick selection or completion. After checking off whether you want the lunch special number 1 through 7, the server can circle french fries, hash browns, or baked potato; sour cream or butter; cole slaw or tossed green; and the type of salad dressing you want—all with a minimum of writing. Your Windows dialog boxes offer you the same advantages since they let you choose all your options from one box.

A number of different elements are used to display and accept information in a dialog box. These elements are tailored to the type of information that you need to provide. For example, a box that you can mark with an X is used when you need to turn a feature on or off. When Windows needs a lengthier description or instruction, a box that accepts text is used. The same elements are employed throughout all dialog boxes in Windows and the applications that you run. Invest a few minutes now in mastering the various components of dialog boxes; it will pay big dividends as you work through this book.

Because dialog boxes bring many options together on one screen, they are ideal candidates for mouse use. You can simply click the options you want to change and bypass the others. With a keyboard, you will need to activate the desired section of the box with a key-combination, and then make your change. Both methods are covered in this chapter. In later chapters, you can decide which method you prefer and use it.

The Components of Dialog Boxes

You will see the following elements in Windows dialog boxes: check boxes, command buttons, drop-down list boxes, list boxes, option buttons, and text boxes. Sometimes several elements are arranged together in group boxes. There are other elements you will see at times, such as messages or display boxes that provide you information. It's important that you learn how to use each of these elements.

Not all dialog boxes contain all possible elements. The options presented

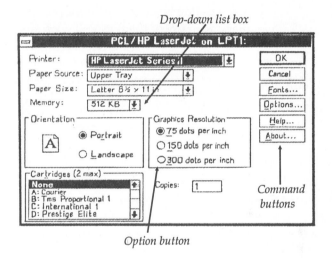

Drop-down list box

Option button

Command buttons

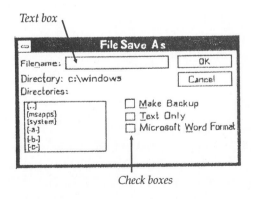

Text box

Check boxes

depend on the choices for the operation and the amount of information that you need to provide. The Program Manager menus show fewer of the dialog box items than you will encounter in the accessory program dialog boxes and in other application programs. The dialog boxes illustrated here are part of the Windows Write accessory.

As on pull-down menus, some dialog box elements may appear dimmed—displayed lighter than the other choices in the menu. When dimmed, these options are not available for your selection.

Using Check Boxes

Check boxes are squares that appear beside "toggle" options; the boxes are empty when the option they represent is not selected (turned off), and marked with an X when the option is selected (turned on). If a dialog box contains multiple check boxes, you can mark as many of them as you wish since they represent independent selections. Think of check boxes as the items on a survey form where you have to check the products that you have used, or on an order form where you have to check the products you want to buy.

4. Which of the following software do you use? (Check all that apply):

☒ WordPerfect
☒ 1-2-3
☐ Excel
☐ dBASE
☒ Harvard Graphics

Note: Selecting a check box always changes its current setting. If a box is blank, selecting it marks it with an X and turns on the option. If a box contains an X, selecting it changes it to a blank box and turns off the option.

To change the current setting for a check box, click it with your mouse; or if you are using a keyboard, press ALT and the underlined letter in the box option. Another keyboard approach is to press TAB until the box is selected, and then press SPACEBAR to mark it or unmark it.

Using Command Buttons

A rectangular button that executes an action for the dialog box is called a *command button*. Command buttons are larger than check boxes, and are labeled with the name of the operation they perform. You will only choose one command button in a dialog box, since any choice excludes the other actions. Think of command buttons as the options on a VCR panel that allow you to fast forward, rewind, play, or record.

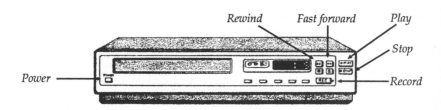

Most dialog boxes in Windows have an OK command button that you can choose to tell Windows to proceed with the operation in question. Another common command button says Cancel, and tells Windows to ignore the current dialog box settings and the fact that you initially requested the command.

If the current dialog box has a default command button selection, the border of the command button is bold. Pressing ENTER automatically selects this option and closes the dialog box.

To choose a command button option with the mouse, all you need to do is click the button. With the keyboard, press ALT and the underlined letter from the command button name.

Using Drop-Down List Boxes

Drop-down list boxes are rectangular boxes that display the default setting for an option, but not all the other alternatives. The presence of an arrow box at the right side of the list box tells you there are other options available. Using this type of box is similar to choosing the name of your county on a

Please Print
Name SAM MATTESON
Address 1215 BRIAN LANE
City GATES MILLS
State OH **Zip** 44128
County CUYAHOGA

See Page 7 for a full County List

survey questionnaire, where the most likely county of residence is listed, and you are directed to another page on the survey form to see the other available counties. The options are available, but not visible on the current page.

Drop-down list boxes give you access to a full range of options in a concise format. To see the other choices, you can use your mouse to click the arrow at the end of the box; then click the desired option in the list that drops down, to replace the current choice. With a keyboard, press ALT and the underlined letter in the list box name to see the available choices; next, press ALT-DOWN ARROW to see the list; then use the arrow keys to highlight the one you want, and press ENTER.

Using List Boxes

List boxes are rectangular boxes that present an entire list of options for a setting. Only one selection from the box is appropriate. If you were choosing a free prize for filling out the survey questionnaire, for example, you might be presented with a list of choices and then be asked to circle the prize you wanted. A list box works the same way.

List boxes that contain a long list of options may have scroll boxes on the right side to facilitate moving quickly through the list. These scroll boxes let you look at options that do not fit in the box. Like the scroll boxes for windows that you learned to use in Chapter 2, you can drag these scroll boxes up or down to move slowly through the list box, or click on the scroll arrows to move quickly through the options.

To select a list box option with a mouse, click it. To select with the keyboard, first activate the list box by pressing ALT and the underlined letter in the list box name. Then use the arrow keys to highlight the desired option, and press ENTER.

Using Option Buttons

Option buttons are round. They have a black center when selected (turned on) and are blank when unselected (turned off). Frequently option buttons are presented in

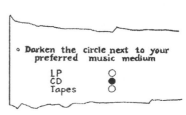

groups, although only one button can be selected. A survey question about your preferred music medium, which lets you select LP, tape, or CD, uses the same concept as option buttons.

You can select, or turn on, an option button by clicking it with a mouse. Selecting one option button in a group turns off all the other buttons in the group. Select another option button, and you turn off the current selection.

To turn on an option button you can click it with a mouse. Or press ALT and the underlined letter in the option name.

Using Text Boxes

Text boxes are rectangular boxes where you can type an entry. Text boxes can be used to enter a filename, the name of a program group, or other, more descriptive information. Some text boxes accept only numbers. On a survey form, a blank entry line would be the equivalent of a text box; you might need to write your name, profession, or company on that entry line.

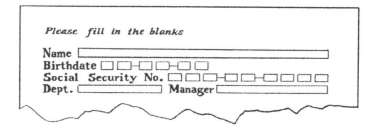

Before you can type an entry in a text box, the I-beam shaped insertion pointer that marks your place on most windows must be in the text box. To move the insertion pointer into the box, click the text box with your mouse. Or activate the text box by pressing ALT and the underlined letter in the text box name. Then type your entry.

Keys to Success

Menus and dialog boxes allow you to tell Windows exactly what you want.

You can use a click of the mouse, or the ALT key plus an underlined letter from the menu name, to pull down a menu. Once it is displayed, you can select options from it by clicking the desired option, or by typing the representative underlined letter from any selection.

To cancel a menu selection, you can press the ESC key or click another area on your screen.

Dialog boxes have many elements that make it easy to set and choose options. These boxes save much of the time needed to move through the multilevel commands used by many non-Windows programs.

What Do They Mean By...?

Check Box   A square box in a dialog box that lists a selection attribute; this attribute can be turned on or off by marking and unmarking the box, with a mouse click or keyboard action.

Command Button   Rectangular buttons labeled with the actions they perform. Only one command button can be chosen at a time in a dialog box, since any choice excludes the other options.

Default   The current setting, which is used if you do not make a change.

Dialog Box   A box that appears in response to a command, that lets you refine the menu option selected. Many different elements can be used to record your selections.

Insertion Point   An I-beam marking your place in a window or text box.

List Box   An element in a dialog box that lists available options, such as files in a directory. Some list boxes drop down to show more alternatives.

Menu Bar   A list of menu options at the top of a window.

Option Buttons   A set of buttons in a dialog box that represent mutually exclusive options. A selected option has a black dot in the center of the button.

Pull-Down Menu   A menu of options that pulls down from a menu bar.

Quick-Key   A combination keystroke that can be used in place of a menu selection.

Text Box   An entry box within a dialog box, where you record more information needed by the menu operation, such as a filename. Some text boxes accept only numbers.

Moving and
Sizing Windows

The ability Windows gives you to use more than one window at a time becomes a real advantage once you master the techniques of moving among windows, as well as changing their location and size. Only you know which windows you want to have on the screen at any time. You also must be the one to decide how much information you want to see in a window and which screen location needs to be the most accessible. Think of your electronic desktop as you do the desktop in your office—to work efficiently, it will be useful to place the desktop accessories and projects you need most often in a location where you will be able to get to them quickly.

There are two different types of windows: *application windows* and *document windows*. Application windows are the windows used for the programs that you are running. Application windows always have a menu bar at the top, which allows you to access commands that are specific to the current application. Document windows, which display within an application window, contain the data you work with. You can have more than one document window open within an application window. Windows offers several ways to arrange the various windows on your desktop, as you'll see in the section "Arranging Windows and Icons," later in this chapter.

The Program Manager and its group windows are examples of application and document group windows. The Program Manager is an application window, which is why it has the name of the application in the title bar and the menu bar below it. The group windows are document windows for the Program Manager. These document windows contain the data the Program Manager works with by containing the other application that you can start. Different applications may call document windows by different names but they are still document windows since they provide the data the application uses. For example, the File Manager that you will learn about in Chapter 8 has document windows called directory windows and search windows. Later in this chapter you will learn how to expand the document window so it fills the remaining space in an application window. When you do this, the document window will seem to be an integrated part of the application window.

Within the Program Manager you can rearrange the icons that represent applications and documents. Windows also provides a special option to "tidy up" a windowful of icons that you may have strewn around on your desktop. You will want to look at the later section, "Arranging Icons," for help with all this.

After spending the time to organize the desktop your way, you will want to save the arrangement so it will be there for your future work sessions. Windows lets you do this when you exit the program, by making a couple of easy settings. You'll see how to do this in "Saving Your Desktop Layout."

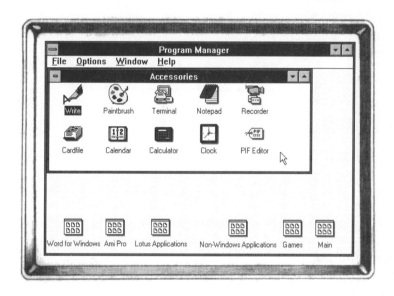

Working with Multiple Windows

Just as you organize your desk a different way each day, depending on the tasks that you need to work on, you may want to do the same thing with your Windows desktop. Some days you will want to open various accessory windows along with application windows. Once you have started a particular application, you might need to have one or more documents open in that application.

Opening Additional Windows

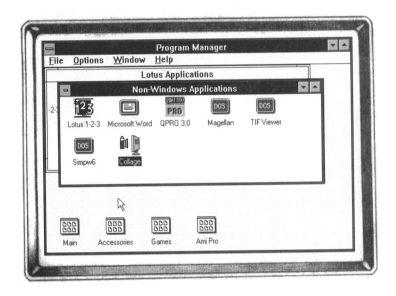

To start an application or open an accessory for use, double-click its icon. You will usually have to first double-click the icon for the group that contains the application or accessory in Program Manager. The program groups where the applications and accessories are stored are shown on document windows called *group windows*. Within the group window, double-click the icon for the specific program you want. If you do not have a mouse handy, you can press CTRL-TAB to move to the group you want. When it is highlighted, press ENTER. Next, use the arrow keys to move to the icon for the application you want to use. When it is highlighted, press ENTER.

Starting from the Program Manager window, try this exercise and open a few group windows and application windows right now:

1. Open the Games window by double-clicking its icon.

Remember: To open an icon, you can move the mouse pointer to the icon and double-click it, or use CTRL-TAB to highlight the icon and press ENTER.

2. Open the Main group icon.

3. Open the Accessories group icon.

Each of the group windows you've opened overlaps the others, forming a stack, with the last window opened (Accessories) on top of the stack.

4. Move the pointer into the Accessories window and double-click on the Write icon. (Or use the LEFT ARROW or RIGHT ARROW key and then press ENTER.) This opens the Write accessory in an application window.

Once the Write window is opened, it obscures the other open windows, as shown just below.

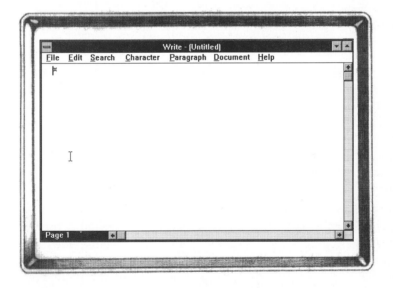

Navigating Among Multiple Windows

Once you have several windows open on the desktop, you will want to be in control of which window is active. You can move among the open windows easily, using either the mouse or keyboard.

Note: First consider whether the window you want to get to is a document or application window, since the technique for moving among the two types of windows is not the same if you use the keyboard. Even if you're using a mouse, there are several selection alternatives available.

Selecting a Specific Window with the Mouse or Keyboard

The easiest way to activate a window, regardless of its type, is to place the mouse pointer somewhere in the window and click it. This window immediately becomes the *active window*. It's like grabbing a project folder and opening it so you can work on its contents. (Of course, you can only use this approach when part of the window is visible.)

When the window that you want to activate is an application window, another way to select it is by using a helpful Windows tool called the Task List. The Task List is a list of all the open application windows. To display the Task List, press CTRL-ESC. Click the task you want to activate, or highlight the task name using the arrow keys and then press ENTER.

Tip: Besides pressing CTRL-ESC you can also display the Task List by clicking the mouse anywhere on the desktop other than in a window. When no window is indicated, the Task List displays for your selection.

When you want to activate a document window, you'll need to move through the stack of open documents until you get to the one you want. If the window is visible, you can click the desired window with your mouse. If not, you need to use the keyboard methods described in the next section.

Moving from Window to Window

If you do not have too many open application and document windows, cycling through all the open windows one by one will be almost as quick as selecting a specific window. This technique is like having a stack of project folders, and moving the top one to the bottom of the stack so you can get to the next folder down. You can continue this to cycle through the folders (and likewise through windows), over and over. When moving among open application windows, Windows uses the order in which the windows were opened to move from window to window.

- To move to the next application window, click the window with a mouse or press ALT-ESC. This activates the next open window that has a menu bar at the top of the window.

- To move to the next document window, press CTRL-TAB, or select the Control Menu document and choose Next.

Moving Among Windows

Once you have several open windows, you will need a technique for controlling which window is the active window. Clicking the window that you want is the easiest solution when you can access even a small corner of the window. You can also press CTRL-TAB to move among document windows, or ALT-ESC to move among application windows. You can also press CTRL-ESC or click part of the screen that does not contain a window to display the Task List. From the Task List, you can select an open application to select the application's window.

Some Keyboard Practice in Moving Among Windows

If you opened all the group and application windows specified earlier in "Opening Additional Windows," you can move among them quickly with the mouse. If you want to try out the keyboard techniques, follow these steps to try a few quick moves:

1. Press ALT-ESC to make the Program Manager window active.

Note: Since Accessories was the last group opened in the Program Manager, the Accessories document (group) window is on the top and highlighted, indicating that it is the active document window in the Program Manager.

2. Press CTRL-TAB to move to the next document (group) window, making Main the active window.

3. Press CTRL-TAB again, making the Games window active.

4. Press CTRL-ESC to display the Task List.

5. Highlight Write and press ENTER.

To close each of the open windows except the Program Manager window, double-click the Control Menu box for each window.

Arranging Windows and Icons

As you open windows, information in existing windows might be obscured by new windows that you open—in much the same way that opening a project folder on your desk may cover up other important papers. When you want to arrange your windows just so, you can create a custom location for each window, or you can let Windows arrange the open windows for you, in one of two different arrangements.

Icons, too, can be moved to new locations—individually, or all at once with a special Windows option.

Arranging Windows

Windows provides two predefined arrangements for open windows, or you can select locations for windows individually. The predefined options are Cascade, which presents a stack of windows with each title bar visible, and Tile, which lays out the windows like floor tiles.

Cascading Windows

A cascade arrangement of open windows places the active window on top of the stack with other open windows *cascading* beneath it, so that the title bar of all the other open windows is visible and accessible to mouse clicks. This arrangement is convenient when you need to see all the information in just one window at a time, but you need to move among and activate different windows frequently.

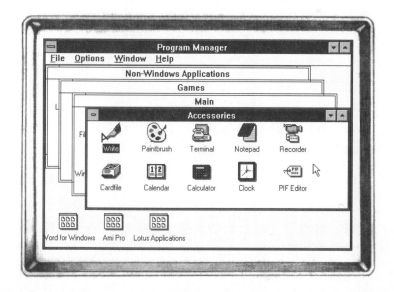

To cascade your open windows, open the Window menu and choose Cascade, or press the SHIFT-F5 quick-key. The window that is active when you make your request will be the one at the top of the stack. Your can cascade all the applications on your desktop by clicking the Cascade button or by pressing ALT-C in the Task List.

Tiling Windows

Tiled windows cover the desktop as linoleum tiles cover a floor. The size of the window tiles will depend on the number of windows that are open when you make the request. All window tiles are equal in size and are arranged in a regular pattern to cover the desktop. A tiled arrangement is useful when you need to see several windows at once but you don't need to see all the information of any one window.

To tile open windows, open the Window menu and choose Tile, or press the SHIFT-F4 quick-key. Windows determines the number of open windows and allots equal space on the screen to each one. You can tile all of the applications on your desktop by clicking the Tile button or by pressing ALT-T in the Task List.

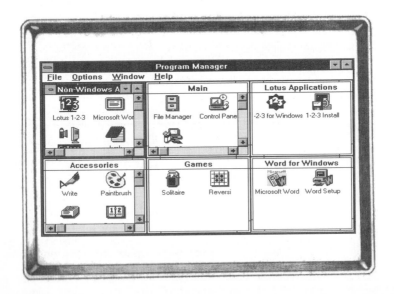

Creating a Custom Window Arrangement

When you create a custom layout of the windows on your desktop, you decide exactly where you want to place each open window. You can move the open windows around and thus create an overlapping pattern that lets you see just the information you need and arrange the windows any way you want.

The easiest way to move a window is to move the mouse pointer to the title bar of the window and drag it to a new location.

Remember: To drag an object, point to it, and then press and hold down the mouse button while you move the mouse across the desktop. When the object is placed where you want it, release the mouse button.

You can also relocate a window using the keyboard. Make the window active, and select Move from the Control Menu. Then use the arrow keys to relocate the window and press ENTER.

Arranging Icons

You can place icons anywhere you want them on the desktop. If you do not have a specific location in mind, you can let Windows "tidy up" the current placement by using the Window Arrange option.

Using the Arrange Option

The Arrange option in the Window menu rearranges all of the icons in the current window. Think of this command as a request for Windows to straighten up a sloppy window, placing the icons in neat rows and columns. You will find the Arrange option especially useful after you have tiled windows or changed their size. You can arrange the application icons on your desktop by clicking the Arrange Icons button or by pressing ALT-A in the Task List.

Custom Icon Placement

If you know exactly where you want to place an icon, you can move it yourself. To move an icon to a new location, simply drag the icon to a new place.

Sizing Windows

Using either the mouse or the keyboard, you can make a window as large as the desktop or as small as its icon, or any size in between. Windows also supplies special boxes in every window that you can click to instantly *maximize* a window to fill up an application window or desktop, or *minimize* a window into an icon.

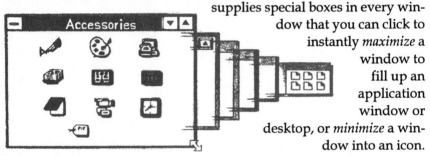

Creating a Custom Window Size

As with most Windows tasks, the mouse provides the easiest technique for changing a window's size. First move the pointer to the border of the window that you want to expand or contract. The mouse changes shape, into a two-headed arrow. After pressing the mouse button, drag inward or outward to make the window smaller or larger.

If you click and drag the corner of the window, you can change two dimensions of the window size at once. Click on any corner, and drag in toward the center of the window, and watch the window's height and width decrease at the same time. Likewise, drag out and away from the center of the window to increase both the height and width.

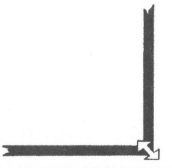

If you must use the keyboard to change the size of your windows, you can choose the Size option from the Control Menu. Then use your arrow keys to indicate the desired window size and press ENTER when you are done.

Minimizing and Maximizing a Window

Windows provides special boxes at the upper-right corner of every window, for minimizing and maximizing a window. These boxes are labeled with arrowheads that point up or down.

The upward-pointing arrow is the Maximize box; click it to enlarge a window. If the window is an application window, the application window will expand to fill the desktop. If the window is a document window, the document window will expand to fill the application window. The document window may have other changes such as the document name appearing as part of the application's title bar and the document's Control Menu box appearing in the application's menu bar. The downward-pointing arrow is the Minimize box; use it to reduce a window of any size to an icon.

You will want to maximize a window when you want to see as much of that window as possible, and minimize a window when you want to keep it active for quick access but also need to have more of the desktop available for other windows.

Although it takes a little longer, you can also choose the Minimize or Maximize options on the Control Menu to make the same changes to your windows.

Restoring a Window to Its Previous Size

When a window is already at its maximum size, the Maximize box is replaced with a Restore box. This box has two arrowheads, pointing up and down.

 Clicking on the Restore box changes the window back to whatever size it was before you maximized it.

To restore a minimized window, double-click its icon, or click the icon and choose Restore.

Saving Your Desktop Layout

When you attempt to exit from Windows, an Exit Windows dialog box appears, asking you to confirm your request. In addition, the dialog box contains a Save Changes check box that allows you to indicate whether you want to save any changes that you made to the desktop settings. If the box is marked with an X, the settings will be saved. You can mark this box by clicking it or by pressing ALT-S to select the box. To unmark the box, just click it or select it again. Then click OK to process your exit request and save your settings.

Note: Once you have marked the Save Changes box to turn on this option, it remains on until you turn it off.

Keys to Success

To open additional windows, double-click the window icon or highlight it and press ENTER.

You can make any open window the active window just by clicking it. Also, to activate an application window, you can press CTRL-ESC or click on an open area of the desktop; this displays the Task List, where you can select the application you want with a mouse click or by highlighting it and pressing ENTER. Move among open application windows by pressing ALT-ESC, and among document windows by pressing CTRL-TAB to activate them.

You can place a window in the desktop location of your choice by dragging the window by its title bar to the new location. Or you can handle this same task by choosing the Move option from the Control Menu. To change the overall arrangement of windows on the desktop, choose Tile or Cascade from the Window menu.

If you want to relocate icons, drag them to new locations on the desktop. Windows will "tidy up" all the icons for you if you choose Arrange from the Window menu.

You can change the size of a window by dragging the window border or corner outward to make it larger or inward to shrink it. Clicking the Minimize, Maximize, and Restore boxes lets you resize a window or change it to an icon and vice versa. If you prefer, you can also choose the Size, Minimize, Maximize, and Restore options from the Control Menu.

You can tell Windows to save your desktop placement and size settings for future sessions. You need to mark the Save Changes check box in the dialog box that appears when you choose Exit from the File menu.

What Do They Mean By...?

Application Window   A window that contains a program that you use to work with data. Application windows have a menu bar, a larger Control Menu box, and the application name in its title bar.

Arranging Icons   Placing icons on the screen in an organized pattern.

Cascading   Creating a stack of open windows, with the title bar from each window visible and the active window on the top.

Document Window   A window that contains the data that you use in an application. This can be information like text, numbers, graphics, or, in the case of the Program Manager, other applications that you can run separately. Document windows have their own Control Menu box and title bar.

Maximizing a Window   Enlarging a window to full desktop size or the size of its application window.

Minimizing a Window   Displaying a window as an icon (its smallest possible size).

Menu Bar   The bar of options at the top of an application window.

Restoring a Window   Enlarging or shrinking a window to return it to its former size.

Sizing a Window   Changing the size of the document window within the application window or of the application window on the Windows desktop.

Task List   A list of the applications that are open in Windows, so you can select which application window you want to work with.

Tiling   Reorganizing open windows so that they are equal in size and arranged like floor tiles.

Title Bar   The bar at the top of the window that contains the name of the window or current filename.

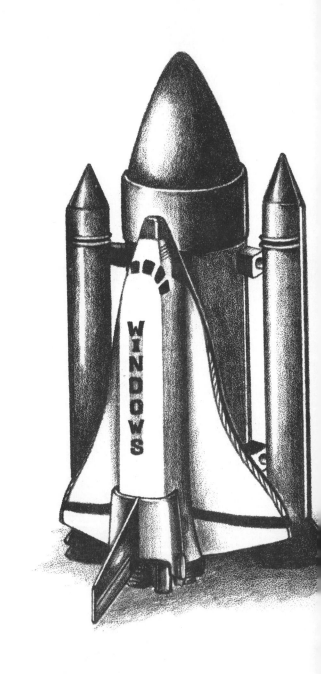

Starting and Using Programs 5

Most of the time when you are using Windows, you will be running programs. In fact, one of the principal advantages offered by Windows is the ability to run (or execute) multiple programs at one time. You might load one program to perform your budget computations, and then start another program that lets you type a memo about how that budget turned out. In Windows both programs can remain active, and you can switch between the two tasks easily.

Windows includes a program launching capability that makes it possible for you to run a program without knowing anything about where the program files are located. Windows keeps track of the files that you need to run your programs, and provides several different ways to start them. The Program Manager has charge of these tasks.

Windows lets you run both Windows-compatible and non-Windows programs. Non-Windows programs are all the applications that are not specifically designed to operate from within Windows. These may be programs that you have had for awhile and have been running under DOS, or recently acquired programs for which there is not yet a Windows version written. Although you can run these programs from within Windows and enjoy some of the advantages of Windows while using them, you will not have the benefit of using all the Windows features.

Most popular Windows-specific application programs share some common menu selections. You will appreciate this consistency as you acquire and learn additional programs, and will find that you are already familiar with some of each new program's features.

Starting a Program

When you *run* (or execute) a program, you are placing the set of instructions that is the program into the memory of your computer. You can then use the features of the program to create budgets, graphs, reports, or memos.

If you tried the examples in Chapter 4, you started a program without realizing it. When you double-clicked the Write icon in the Accessories window, the Write program was started. In this chapter you will explore the full set of options for starting programs. In addition to using an icon in the Program Manager to start a program, you can also use a *command* in either the Program Manager or the File Manager—although this means you need to do a bit of typing. You can also select the name of the program file in the File Manager to start a program. It may seem surprising to have so many options for starting a program, but if you think about it, you'll realize that you usually have alternatives for most manual tasks, too. For a task as simple as turning on your television set you can use the On/Off button on the set or on a remote control device, or you can ask someone else to turn the set on for you.

Using the Icons in the Program Manager

You can have Windows add all of your programs to *program groups*. Program groups are nothing more than documents that contain icons for application programs or even other program groups. If you allowed Windows to set up your applications for you after installation, you now have program groups for Windows Applications and Non-Windows Applications. You also probably have other groups of related programs. In Chapter 7 you will learn how to create your own program groups, as well as how to add programs that Windows cannot set up in groups for you automatically.

As you look at the icons on your Program Manager screen, you'll see that each of the icons clearly represents a group of programs. If you open the Games program group, it displays the icons for several game programs. Accessories contains icons for all the desktop accessories that Windows provides. The use of program groups keeps the Program Manager window uncluttered, yet makes it clear where you can look to find a program. Later you may find that some of your applications get used frequently enough and have a sufficient number of related programs and files to warrant setting them up as a separate group on their own.

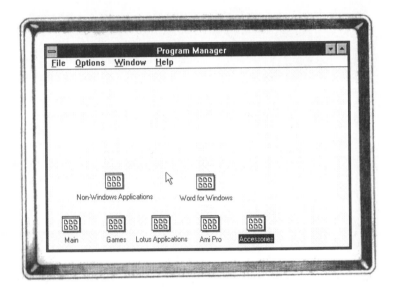

To run a program in any group, double-click the icon for the desired group, or select it and press ENTER. Then double-click the icon for the program itself, or select it and press ENTER.

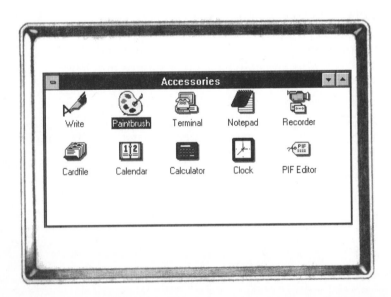

Running a Program from Its Icon

To run a program within a program group:

1. Double-click the icon for the program group in the Program Manager, or highlight the icon and press ENTER.

2. When the program group opens, double-click the icon for the program itself, or highlight the desired program icon and press ENTER.

Let's try this feature by opening the Calculator accessory. First open the Accessories window. Remember—double-clicking the group icon (or highlighting it and pressing ENTER) is how you open program group icon. Next, double-click the Calculator icon (or highlight it and press ENTER).

To close the Calculator window, you can press ALT-SPACEBAR and select Close.

Using Run from the Program Manager or File Manager

Applications that you use frequently should be available as icons, so you can start them quickly. In Chapter 7 you'll learn how to set up your favorite applications as icons (if they aren't already). For applications used less often, you may find it just as easy to use the Run command in the Program or File Manager.

To start a program from either the Program Manager or File Manager, you must run the program. You know that one way to do this is to use the program's icon, but here you will learn how to run a program by specifying its filename.

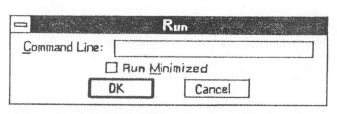

Filenames for programs have an .EXE or .COM filename extension. Filenames for files that are capable of launching programs in Windows have a .PIF or .BAT extension.

If you want, you can also open a *data file* when you start the program. A data file contains information, such as a memo, graph, or budget report, that the program works with. Data files have filename extensions different from program files; these extensions vary widely, depending on the program that created the file.

As you know, the Program Manager is available as soon as you start Windows. To access the File Manager, however, you must first open the Main program group (with a double-click of the mouse or by selecting the icon and pressing ENTER). You can then double-click the File Manager icon (or highlight it and press ENTER). Despite the differences between the File Manager and Program Manager menus, you can use the same keystrokes to run a program from either menu.

WP Directory

MEMO
RPT 1
RPT 2

ACCT Directory

BUDGET
SALES 1
SALES 2

When it starts a program for you, Windows keeps track of the location of the program files that you need. This location information is called the *path*, and usually includes a drive letter name, followed by directory names. Windows maintains location information for all the programs that are part of all program groups. These location specifications are important, because there can be thousands of files on a disk. You've learned that directories are listings of where to look for a group of files that have some similarities. Directories make it possible to find a file without searching the entire disk.

When you access a program with the Run command, it is often necessary to provide the path information yourself. (If the files that you need are in the current directory, you do not need to specify their location.) Also, it is possible that you may have used a PATH statement in the startup file for your system (AUTOEXEC.BAT) telling your system to look in locations other than the current directory.

Note: If you try to run a program and Windows cannot find it, your next step should be to enter the location of the file along with the filename in the text box for the Run command. For instance, if you want to run a program called WP on the C drive in the WP51 directory, you would need to enter C:\WP51\WP *in the Run command text box.*

To run a program from the File Manager or Program Manger menu, follow these steps:

1. Choose Run from the File menu of either File Manager or Program Manager.

2. Type the name of the program (the filename) in the Command Line text box. Remember that you need to include the path for the file in most cases.

3. If you want to open a data file, too, press the SPACEBAR after you type the program name/path, and then type the name of the data file, with its path, if needed.

4. Click OK or press ENTER.

For example, to run the program WP.EXE from the WP51 directory on drive C, and open the data file MEMO in the WPDATA directory on drive D, your entry in the Command Line text box would be:

C:\WP51\WP D:\WPDATA\MEMO

Running a Program from Program Manager or File Manager

The Program Manager automatically displays on your screen when you start Windows, but you must open the File Manager to use it to run a program. Open the Main program group, and then open File Manager. With either Program Manager or File Manager active, follow these steps:

1. Choose Run from the File menu of either Program Manager or File Manager.

2. In the Command Line text box, type the name of the program that you want to run. If you want to open a data file after starting the program, add a space and then type the name of the file. If a file is not located in the current directory, you need to precede the filename with a drive and directory specification.

3. Choose OK or press ENTER.

Running a Minimized Program

The Run command in the File menu of the Program Manager and File Manager lets you run an application as a *minimized program*, that is, as an icon rather than a window. If you mark the Run Minimized check box in the Run dialog box, the program shrinks to an icon as soon as it starts. "Running minimized" is like having a hidden worker perform tasks for you while you are working on other things. Just as you can check with the worker for a status report on his or her task, you can always enlarge (maximize) the minimized icon and get a closer look at its task in that application's window. To maximize a minimized icon, just double-click it at any time.

Selecting the Filename in the File Manager

The last alternative for starting a program is to use its directory listing within the File Manager. You'll learn more about the File Manager in Chapter 8, but for now all you need to master is how to select a filename from the File Manager's many lists of files.

Remember: The File Manager lists filenames; this list differs from the Task List, which shows active programs.

The File Manager's directory listing is designed to allow you to move quickly though the contents of any of your disks. To open any directory, all you need to do is double-click the directory name. After identifying a file with the appropriate filename and extension, you can start the program associated with the file by double-clicking the filename, or highlighting it and choosing Open from the File menu.

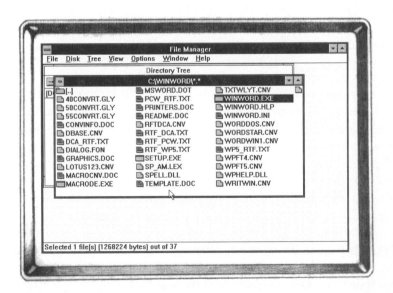

Starting a Program from the File Manager

Another way of starting a program is to select the filename from the
File Manager's directory listing, as follows:

1. Open the File Manager.

2. Double-click the drive and/or directory where the file
   is stored.

3. Double-click the name of the program file.

If you prefer to use the keyboard, you can use the same alternative of
highlighting the drive, directory, and filename and pressing ENTER
that you have used for previous tasks.

Getting Familiar with the Windows Program Options

Although Windows runs both Windows and non-Windows programs,
there are a number of advantages to using Windows-compatible programs.
For instance, it is easy to share data between these programs.

Moreover, it is easier to learn new programs after you've initially mastered one, since many of the menu commands are identical. (This fact is true of the larger applications, and does not pertain to smaller programs such as the various accessories, many of which have limited menus.) Rather than each program presenting a unique learning experience, you can benefit from everything you already know when you use a new program. It is somewhat like driving a car—once you have learned how to drive an automatic, you know where the gas pedal and brake are located. And you can usually find the odometer and other important gauges in a common location. If you need to drive a different vehicle, you might need to learn some new things (like operating a stick-shift transmission), but you'll immediately feel familiar with most parts of the new vehicle because it has some of the same options as other cars.

The File Menu in Windows Applications

The File menu in most Windows applications provides options for opening files, saving files, printing, and exiting. Some of the File menu options that you are likely to find are listed here:

Command	Function
New	Opens a new document window
Open	Opens an existing document file
Close	Closes the active document window
Save	Saves the active document under its current name
Save As	Saves the active document under a new name or location you specify
Preview	Lets you view printed output on the screen
Print	Prints information from the active document
Printer Setup	Lets you modify printer settings
Exit	Exits from the application program

The Edit Menu in Windows Applications

The Edit menu in Windows applications provides options for copying and moving data to and from the Windows Clipboard. The Clipboard is a temporary storage area to hold data that you copy, cut, and paste among your documents. It is the Clipboard that makes it easy to transfer data between the various applications, because you can cut data or make a copy of data from a file in one application and paste the data into a file in another application. The Clipboard is covered in more detail in Chapter 6.

The Edit menu options that you are likely to find in Windows applications are listed here:

Command	Function
Undo	Reverses the effect of an action
Cut	Removes selected text from the current document and places it on the Clipboard

Copy   Places a copy of selected text from the current
                    document on the Clipboard

Paste   Places the contents of the Clipboard at the pointer
                    location in the current document

Quitting a Program

When you quit or close a
program, you remove it
from memory. To do this
you can press ALT-F4, or
double-click the Control
Menu box. Another way to
quit an application is to
close the application
window. Choose Exit from
the File menu to use this
approach.

If the data that you have
created with the program has not been saved before you exit, you will be
prompted to indicate your wish to save the data or not.

Keys to Success

You have three choices for starting a program: You can double-click the
program icon in the Program Manager. Or you can choose Run from the
File menu in either the Program Manager or File Manager, and then type
the name of the program. Another option is to select the name of the
program file from the File Manager directory list.

Most of the major applications written for Windows contain some standard Windows conventions that make it easy for you to learn new applications once you have mastered one application. You'll find almost identical
options in menus such as File and Edit across all applications. This means

that whether you want to open a graph, memo, or budget, you can choose Open from the File menu—regardless of the program you are using.

You can quit most programs by choosing Exit from the File menu, or pressing ALT-F4.

What Do They Mean By...?

Data File   A file that contains your information, such as a memo or graph you may have created.

Minimized Program   An active program represented by an icon rather than a window while it is running.

Path   The directions for locating a file including its drive and directory.

Program   A set of stored instructions for performing tasks.

Program Group   A group of programs whose icons appear in a program group window.

Run   To place the instructions for a program in memory and begin executing them.

Using the Clipboard

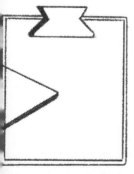

Windows has a special feature called the Clipboard that you can use in most Windows applications. You can take information from any application, store it on the Clipboard, and then put it somewhere else. Once the information is on the Clipboard, you can copy it most anywhere—you can place it in another location of the original application, or into an entirely different application.

The Clipboard lets you share data among files and applications. Suppose you are preparing a budget report. You can use the Clipboard to copy data from your budget spreadsheets into the budget report stored in your word processor. The Clipboard can hold many types of data, so you can store spreadsheet numbers, graphics, and text, and then share them with any application that will accept the Clipboard's data.

Most of the time you will not look in the Clipboard file itself, but will simply transfer data to and from it. Though Windows does have a Clipboard application program, it is not necessary that you use this application to use the Clipboard. The Clipboard application allows you to view the contents of the Clipboard without changing its contents.

How the Clipboard Works

The Clipboard is actually a temporary "holding area" in memory that Windows uses for storing whatever type of data you send to it. The data that you put on the Clipboard remains there until you replace it with some other data, or until you exit Windows.

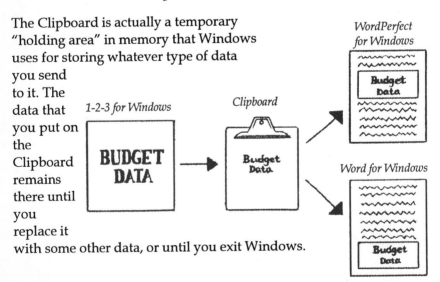

Windows applications make it easy for you to use the Clipboard because most of them use the same commands for Clipboard-related operations. Most Windows applications that can use the Clipboard have an Edit menu that contains options like Copy, Cut, and Paste.

- When you use Copy, the information you select in an application's file is placed on the Clipboard, and left untouched in its original location. This is like copying a recipe from a book; you have the copy on a new sheet of paper, and it also remains in the book.

- The Cut option removes the selected data from its original location and moves (cuts) it to the Clipboard. The Cut option is the same as if you clipped some football scores from the newspaper; the scores are no longer in the paper for others to read, but you have them on the cutting in your hand.

- Paste copies the information you have placed on the Clipboard into a file in the current application, at the current location of the insertion point. Some applications have a Paste Special command with options for specifying how the Clipboard data is copied to the application. In an application such as a spreadsheet, for example, Paste Special might allow you to copy the format of a Clipboard entry without copying the entry itself. Since pasting data to an application does not remove the data from the Clipboard, you can copy the data on the Clipboard again and again to other locations.

 Just as you can take the recipe you copied or the scores you clipped and paste them to another piece of paper, you can also paste Clipboard data, regardless of whether you cut it or copied it.

The Cut, Copy, and Paste options on the Edit menu have the following quick-key equivalents that you can use in place of the menu options:

CTRL-INS = Copy
SHIFT-DEL = Cut
SHIFT-INS = Paste

If the application you are using has these shortcuts, they will appear next to their respective commands in the Edit menu.

Storing Data on the Clipboard

The first step in using the Clipboard is to cut or copy data to it. You can select text, graphics, or a combination of the two. Your application determines how you select the data. Most Windows applications let you select the data you will cut or copy. This usually means dragging the mouse over the text or entries you want to cut or copy. For many applications that work with text, you can hold down the SHIFT key as you move through the data to select text.

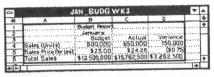

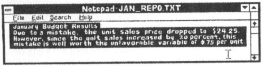

Once you have selected the data, choose Copy from the Edit menu if you want to place a copy of the selection on the Clipboard, and let the original data remain in its current location; or choose Cut from the Edit menu if you want the data removed from its original location and placed on the Clipboard. When you execute either command, the selected data is entered on the Clipboard. Now let's examine the process for getting the data from the Clipboard to another location.

Pasting Data from the Clipboard

Once the Clipboard contains data, you can insert it in other locations in the same application or in different applications. Before you paste the data, you will want to move to the place in the application file where you want the copy of the data to be placed. This usually means positioning the cursor or insertion point in that place. Once you select a location, choose Paste in the Edit menu.

Different applications receive the Clipboard contents into a file in various ways. For example, if you copy spreadsheet data into a word processor, the data from the spreadsheet columns is usually separated by tab characters in its new location. If you copy a graphic image from the Clipboard into an application, the image may look different depending on how the application handles graphics.

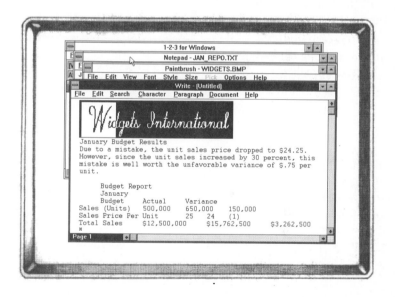

Opening the Clipboard Application

If you ever want to look at the current contents of the Clipboard, you can open the Clipboard application. This application also lets you save the Clipboard's contents to a file, in case you want to reenter those contents on the Clipboard at a later time.

To open the Clipboard application, open the Main program group by double-clicking Main in the Program Manager; then double-click the Clipboard icon. Windows opens the Clipboard, and displays a window containing the current contents of the Clipboard, like this one:

You cannot alter the data within this Clipboard window. You can, however, delete the contents by choosing Delete in the Edit menu. Frequently you will want to save the contents to a file, or open another Clipboard file and replace the Clipboard's current contents with the contents of that file, as described in the boxed text below.

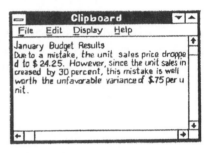

Closing the Clipboard is just like exiting other Windows applications. You can double-click the Clipboard's Control Menu box, or you can press ALT-F4. If you prefer to use a menu, select File and choose Exit. Closing the Clipboard does not remove the contents of the Clipboard; it only closes the

Opening and Closing the Clipboard Application

When you want to open the Clipboard to view its current contents, you can open the Clipboard just like you open other applications. Double-click Main in the Program Manager; then double-click the Clipboard icon.

Once the Clipboard is open, you can close it by pressing ALT-F4 or choosing Exit from the File menu. Closing the Clipboard does not remove the data you have put on the Clipboard.

window that displays the current Clipboard's contents.

Exiting Windows also closes the Clipboard, and it does remove the Clipboard's contents. The Clipboard's contents are not retained from one Windows session to the next. To use the contents of the Clipboard in the next Windows session, you have to save the contents to a file, as explained next.

Saving the Clipboard's Contents to a File

The Clipboard has two limitations, but they are easily overcome by simply saving the Clipboard's contents to a file. These limitations are as follows:

- First, the Clipboard can only contain one piece of data at a time—regardless of whether the data is a single paragraph, a piece of a graphic image, or all of a 20-page report. Saving the Clipboard's contents to a file lets you work among various pieces of a greater unit of data.

- Also, the Clipboard's contents remain available only during the current Windows session. When you exit Windows, the Clipboard's contents are erased. To make the Clipboard's contents available the next time you use Windows, save them to a file; then you can bring that file into the Clipboard again in the next Windows session.

To save the Clipboard's contents to a file, open the Clipboard application and choose Save As in the File menu. Type a filename of up to eight characters that Windows will use to store this information on disk, and select OK. Windows saves the Clipboard data to a file with the name you entered

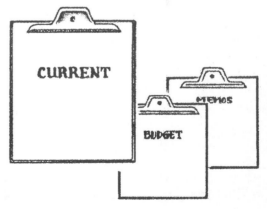

and adds a .CLP extension. When you want to bring a Clipboard file into the Clipboard, choose Open in the Clipboard's File menu, select the appropriate .CLP file from the Files list box, and choose OK. This process replaces the current Clipboard contents with the information stored in the .CLP file.

Using the Clipboard with Non-Windows Applications

Transferring data using the Clipboard with non-Windows applications is not as easy as using the Clipboard with Windows applications, because non-Windows programs were not designed with the Clipboard in mind, and they don't have the Edit menu options needed to easily work with the Clipboard. Nevertheless, you can use the Clipboard to transfer information between non-Windows applications, or between non-Windows and Windows applications. This lets you transfer data between applications that have incompatible file formats.

The way you copy data to and from the Clipboard with non-Windows applications also depends on whether you are running Windows in 386 enhanced mode, or in real or standard mode. The choice of mode will depend

Windows running in REAL MODE less than 1MB RAM

Windows running in 386 Enhanced mode

Windows running in Standard mode

on the type of computer and how much memory you have. If you are copying data from a non-Windows application with Windows in real or standard mode, that application must be in ASCII text mode.

Windows in 386 Enhanced Mode

When copying to the Clipboard with non-Windows applications while running Windows in 386 enhanced mode, you can select onscreen the data that you will copy to the Clipboard.

To copy data from a non-Windows application to the Clipboard when you are running Windows in 386 enhanced mode, first press ALT-ENTER to switch the non-Windows application from running in a full screen to running in a window. Next, select Edit from the non-Windows application window's Control Menu, and choose Mark. Then drag the mouse to highlight the data you want to copy to the Clipboard; or, with the keyboard, use the arrow keys to move the cursor to the beginning of the data you want to copy, and press SHIFT and the arrow keys to highlight the data to copy. To copy the selected data to the Clipboard, press ENTER. Finally, press ALT-ENTER again to return to a full-screen display. Now that the data is in the Clipboard, you can copy it to a Windows application as described previously or to another non-Windows application as described below.

You can paste data on the Clipboard into a non-Windows application regardless of whether the data comes from a Windows or non-Windows application. To paste the Clipboard data into a non-Windows application, first move the cursor or insertion point to the location in the file where you want to place the Clipboard's data. Next, press ALT-ENTER to switch the non-Windows application from full-screen to a window. Select Edit from the application window's Control Menu, and choose Paste. This inserts the information into the non-Windows application just as if you were typing it. Finally, press ALT-ENTER again to return to a full-screen display.

Using Clipboard with Non-Windows Applications and Windows in 386 Enhanced Mode

1. Press ALT-ENTER to switch the non-Windows application from full-screen to a window.

2. Select Edit and choose Mark from the application's Control Menu.

3. Drag the mouse to highlight the data you want to copy to the Clipboard.

4. Press ENTER to copy the selected data to the Clipboard.

5. Press ALT-ENTER again to return to a full-screen display.

6. Switch to the application or document where you want the Clipboard's data copied, and move the cursor/insertion point to where you want the data inserted.

7. Press ALT-ENTER to switch the application from full-screen to a window.

8. Select Edit and choose Paste from the application window's Control Menu.

9. Press ALT-ENTER again to return to a full-screen display.

Note: If you are transferring data from a Windows application to a non-Windows application, copy the Windows data into the Clipboard with Edit Copy or Cut, and then perform steps 6 through 8 above. If you are transferring data from a non-Windows application to a Windows application, follow steps 1 through 6 above, and then paste the Clipboard data to the Windows application with Edit Paste.

Windows in Real or Standard Mode

If you are copying to and from the Clipboard with non-Windows applications while running Windows in real/standard mode, you will need to copy the entire screen in order to transfer data to the Clipboard, and have Windows type (paste) the contents of the Clipboard into the non-Windows application. As a reminder, the non-Windows application must be running in text mode to copy data to the Clipboard.

To paste the Clipboard data into a non-Windows application when you are using Windows in real/standard mode, you will paste the entire screen onto the Clipboard. First, move the cursor/insertion point within the document so that the data you want to copy to the Clipboard appears on the screen. Next, press PRINT SCREEN. This copies all of the information on the screen onto the Clipboard, including application-specific elements like titles, menus, and borders. Once this data is on the Clipboard, you can copy it into another application and strip out the information you do not want.

Tip: If PRINT SCREEN *does not work, try* SHIFT-PRINT SCREEN *or* ALT-PRINT SCREEN.

To paste the Clipboard data into a file in a non-Windows application with Windows running in real/standard mode, first move the cursor/insertion point to the location in the document where you want to paste the Clipboard's data. Next, press CTRL-ESC to switch to the Task List, and display the non-Windows application as an icon at the bottom of the desktop. Click the icon once to display the non-Windows application's Control Menu, and choose Paste. This pastes the information from the Clipboard into the non-Windows application just as if you were typing it.

Keys to Success

The Clipboard lets you transfer data between applications and copy data into multiple other locations. The Clipboard is an area of memory Windows reserves for temporarily storing any data you want it to. Once data is on the Clipboard, you can copy it within the same application, or into other applications, both Windows and non-Windows.

Using Clipboard with Non-Windows Applications and Windows in Real or Standard Mode

1. Adjust the display of your file in the non-Windows application so that you can see all of the data you want to copy to the Clipboard.

2. Press PRINT SCREEN to copy the screen to the Clipboard.

3. Switch to the application or document to which you want the data pasted, and move to where you want the data inserted.

4. Press CTRL-ESC to display the Task List.

5. Click the non-Windows application's icon once to display the application's Control Menu.

6. Choose Paste from the non-Windows application window's Control Menu.

Note: If you are transferring data from a Windows application to a non-Windows application, copy the Windows data onto the Clipboard with Edit Copy or Cut, and then perform steps 3 through 6 above. If you are transferring data from a non-Windows application to a Windows application, follow steps 1 through 3 above, and then paste the Clipboard data to the Windows application with Edit Paste.

You use options on the Windows Edit menu to put data onto the Clipboard and to paste data from the Clipboard to the application. Most Windows applications use these same Edit menu options.

There is also a separate Clipboard application in the Main group window of the Program Manager. When you open this application, you can view but not alter the contents of the Clipboard file. The most common reason for opening the Clipboard application is to save the Clipboard's contents to a file, or to transfer a file's contents onto the Clipboard.

Non-Windows applications do not transfer data to and from the Clipboard in the same manner as do Windows applications. The way non-Windows applications translate data to/from the Clipboard depends on whether Windows is running in 386 enhanced mode, or in real or standard mode.

What Do They Mean By...?

386 Enhanced Mode   The mode in which Windows runs if you have a computer with an 80386 processor and at least one megabyte of memory. In this mode, both Windows and non-Windows applications can run within windows on the desktop.

Clipboard   A section of memory that Windows uses to store data from Windows and non-Windows applications so you can share data between applications.

Non-Windows Applications   Application programs that were not designed specifically to run with Windows.

Real Mode   The running mode for Windows on an older computer or a computer with less than one megabyte of memory. You can run only one program at a time because memory space is limited.

Standard Mode   The running mode for Windows in a computer with an 80286 processor and at least one megabyte of memory. Although you can run multiple applications in this mode, non-Windows applications must run in a full screen, rather than a window.

Windows Applications   Application programs designed to run under Windows.

Exploring the
Program
Manager

7

By now you have gained some experience with the Program Manager, and with a little continued practice you will begin to feel like a real pro. So far you have been using Program Manager to start programs, and are probably getting familiar with the various group icons and windows that appear when you use it.

In this chapter you are going to learn more about program groups. You will see how to set up your own groups as a way of keeping similar application programs together, and how to move programs from one group to another. You will also learn about the special program information (.PIF) files that Windows uses to run non-Windows applications.

This is the chapter that shows you the inner workings of the Program Manager. At this point you know how to utilize the tools that the Program Manager provides, but you are about to become a program group construction expert.

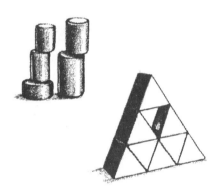

The Organizing Role of the Program Manager

Because of its program group structure, the Program Manager makes it easy to find the program that you need, and to start a program. A *program group* contains the names and icons for one or more related programs. When you first install Windows, the number of program groups that you have depends on the programs that are on your hard disk. If you have installed a number of different application programs, the groups that you are likely to have are Main, Accessories, Games, Windows Applications, and non-Windows Applications.

What is inside?

Just by looking at the initial groups that Windows provides, you can easily see that you should look in the Games group if you are looking for a game called Solitaire, and the Accessories group if you are looking for a calculator. Some of the other groups have names that are not so explicit. Until you have opened these groups a few times and become familiar with their contents, you might feel as if you are working with cans that have no labels, because the group names do not say exactly what you'll find.

- The Windows and non-Windows Application groups contain exactly what their names indicate. In the Windows group are all the programs specifically designed to run with Windows and utilize all of its features. In the non-Windows Applications group are the programs on your computer that were not specifically designed for Windows.

- The Main group contains the Windows utilities. Here you will find the program that sets up the colors of your Windows screen; a print utility called Print Manager that handles all your printed output; the Clipboard that facilitates the transfer of information between files and applications; and other programs.

Most Windows applications that you purchase handle the task of setting up their own program group. They also place within that group the various programs that are part of the application, so you can execute any of them from an icon. Applications that do not create these groups and icons for you are more difficult to access. For them you will need to use the Run command in the Program Manager's File menu, and type in the name of the application that you want to run.

In Program Manager you can even create your own groups, so you can access any program that you have by simply double-clicking its icon rather than using the Run command. You may also want to create new *group windows*, to better organize programs that are currently part of other groups.

Tip: You will need to create a new group window when you want to create a new category for storing programs and documents. Another time you will want to create a new group is when the number of programs in an existing group approaches 40. With this many program icons in a group window, it makes sense to split the group into two or more different groups.

Creating New Groups

To create a new program group, follow these steps:

1. Activate the Program Manager window.

2. Choose New from the Program Manager's File menu, which displays the New Program Object dialog box.

3. Notice that this dialog box contains option buttons for creating a new program group as well as a new program item. (A *program item* represents the program stored in it.) To tell Windows that you want to create a program group, choose the Program Group button, making the dialog box look like this:

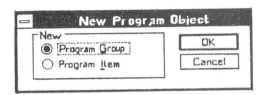

4. Choose the OK button.

5. Now that you have told Windows to create a new group, you need to define it in the dialog box that appears next. At a minimum, this means giving the group a name by entering it in the Description text box, as shown below, up to 25 characters:

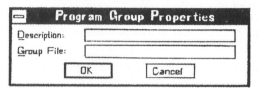

For example, if you type **Games for One** in the Description text box and choose OK, a group by that name is created.

Although you can also complete the Group File text box with a DOS filename to provide a location for the information on the group, Windows does this for you if you leave the box blank. Typically you will not care what filename is used, so you might as well save some work and leave the box blank.

6. Choose the OK button.

Creating a New Program Group

To create a new program group, make Program Manager active and choose New from the File menu. From the New Program Object dialog box, select Program Group and then OK. In the next dialog box, specify a Description to be used for the name of the program group window or its icon when minimized. Choose OK to finalize the procedure.

Adding Items to a Program Group

Program groups can contain program items. As explained earlier in the chapter, a program item is the name and icon used to represent a program that is part of a group. Let's take a look at how to add program items to a group in Program Manager.

Games for One

You can add program items to a group to represent new application programs that may not have been on your disk when you installed Windows. Or you can add program items that already exist in other groups. Even if a program is in another group, you can move its icon to a different group, or you can make a copy of its icon in another group. When you copy a program item, Windows does not copy the program itself, but only the name and icon, thus allowing you to access the program from two different groups.

Moving and Copying Items

When you want to restructure your program groups, you can move and copy program items among the various groups that you have set up. Perhaps you have too many programs in an existing group; you can create a new group, and then move some of the program items from the overcrowded group to the new one. When you want to be able to access a program from multiple groups, you'll want to copy it to all those groups, rather than move it. For example, you might have a group named Accounting for all the applications that you use in your accounting work; you might also need to have one of the programs in this group available from another group, such as the Payroll group.

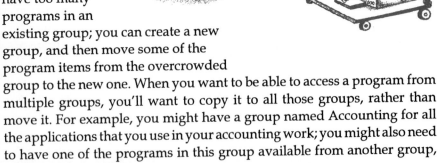

To move a program item from one group to another, simply drag the icon for the program into the group window where you want it. You can make this process even easier by tiling both the old and new group windows so that you can view both at the same time. To move the Solitaire program, for instance, from the Games group to the Games for One group, all you need to do is drag its icon to the new location.

Since you are not limited to accessing a program item from one group only, you may find it convenient to add icons for your most frequently used applications to several program groups. To copy an icon rather than move it, all you need to do is press the CTRL key and hold it down while you are dragging the program icon. Returning to our Solitaire example, to copy the Solitaire program icon so that it appears in the Games for One group as well as the Games group, hold the CTRL key down as you drag the Solitaire icon from the Games window to the Games for One window.

Moving and Copying Items Among Program Groups

To move a program item to a different group, drag its icon into the new group window. To copy a program item, hold down CTRL while you drag the icon to the new group window.

Creating a New Item

New program items are often added to a group window as the new application is installed. If the application's installation procedure supports this automatic addition, the program item can be added to a group automatically. If installation does not set up the program item for you, you will have to add it yourself if you want to start the program from a group window. To do this, you need to tell Windows what entry needs to be made on the command line to start the program, as explained just below.

To create a new Windows program item:

1. Activate the Program Manager window.

2. Select the group window to which you want the program item added.

3. Choose New from the File menu.

4. In the New Program Object dialog box, select Program Item and OK. You'll see this Program Item Properties dialog box:

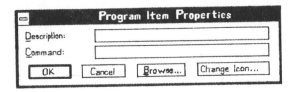

5. In the Description text box, type the description (name) that you want to use for the program icon.

6. In the Command Line text box, enter the command that you want to use to start the program.

The Command Line entry is the command that you would use to start the program with the Run command in the File menu, from either the File Manager or the Program Manager. It is this command that will be executed when you double-click the program icon you are adding. If you are not certain of the name of the program file or its location, you can choose the Browse button to look at the names of all the program files on your disk.

7. Choose OK to add the program item.

Deleting Items and Groups

If you have created a program item that you no longer want, you do not have to keep it. You can delete program items for programs you no longer use, as well as the program items that also appear in another group window. When you delete a program item, you only delete the connection Windows creates between the icon and the application it starts; you can still start a program without an icon.

Creating a New Program Item

Note: You probably will not need to create many new program items, because most application installation procedures take care of this task for you. Some even set up a new program group for the various program items that belong to an application.

When you do need to add a program item, activate the group window in the Program Manager to which you want the program item added. Next, choose New from the File menu. In the New Program Object dialog box, choose Program Item and OK. Then specify a description (in the Program Item Properties dialog box) to be used for the program name in the group window or for its icon when minimized, as well as a command line that will be executed when you select the program item. Choose the OK button to finalize the procedure.

If you want to try deleting a program item, first make certain you are still in the Games for One group, so you don't accidentally change any of Windows's default group setups. To delete a program item, activate the group window affected (in this case, Games for One), and select the program item to delete. Then open the File menu and choose Delete. Notice in the File menu that you can also execute this option by pressing DEL.

Before Windows deletes the item, you are prompted to confirm your request, as shown here:

In this dialog box, select Yes to delete this item from the active program group, which is Games for One. (Remember that Solitaire is also in the Games group, so you will still be able to start Solitaire in the Games window.)

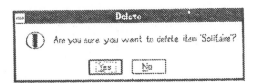

Deleting program groups is just as easy. Before you delete a group, remove all of the program items in the group window. Next, choose Delete in the Program Manager's File menu. Because you have deleted all the group's program items, Windows now assumes that you want to delete the group. Just as when you deleted a program item, Windows prompts you for a confirmation before removing the group. You must select Yes to execute the deletion.

Using Windows Setup to Create Groups and Program Items

To make it easy to add programs to groups, Windows provides an application setup program that adds applications to program groups for you. You probably have already used this application as part of the process of installing Windows. To use this program now, you need to activate the Main program group and select the Windows Setup program item. Open the Options menu and choose Set Up Applications. You'll see this Set Up Applications dialog box:

As indicated in the dialog box, you can have Windows check all of your drives for applications, in the directories listed in your 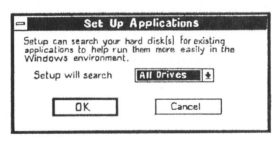 computer's PATH statement (where DOS looks for files), or any other drive/directory. You can select from the drop-down list box to change the drives/directories that are searched. When you are ready for the search to begin, choose OK.

After searching your disk, Windows displays a second Set Up Applications dialog box.

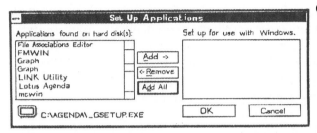

On the left you'll see a scrollable list of all of the applications found on your hard disk. To have Windows set up an application, select the application and then click the Add button. To add all the applications Windows finds on the disk, click the Add All button; you can always delete the ones you do not want later.

The applications you select for Windows to add are removed from the list on the left and placed in the list on the right. When you've moved all desired applications to the list on the right, choose the OK button. Windows then adds your chosen applications to the Windows Applications and Non-Windows Applications groups (it will first create these groups, if necessary). Once the applications are added, you are returned to the Windows Setup window that you started with. You can leave this window and return to the Program Manager by choosing Exit in the Options menu.

A Note About Setting Up Non-Windows Applications

Since non-Windows programs are not specifically designed to run under Windows, you need to tell Windows what computer resources it must provide for the application to run. Most non-Windows applications include a *program information file*, with a .PIF filename extension, that contains the application's requirements. (It may need a specific amount of conventional, expanded, or extended memory, for example, or exclusive use of a printer or a communications port.)

Windows contains a .PIF file called _DEFAULT.PIF; this file is used when a non-Windows application does not have its own .PIF file. Your computer may have .PIF files from three other sources: Many applications include the .PIF file with their program files, which you can copy into your Windows directory. When you have Windows set up applications for you, Windows will create .PIF files for some of the more popular applications, such as Lotus 1-2-3 and WordPerfect. A third source is you, when you create .PIF files using the PIF Editor in the Accessories group window. This option is used when you want to create a custom .PIF file for an application, or when you want to modify an existing one. Most of the time, however, you will use the default .PIF file in Windows or the one that comes with the application.

To have an application use a .PIF file other than _DEFAULT.PIF, you select the specific .PIF file in place of the executable program (.EXE) file in the Command Line text box of the Program Item Properties dialog box. If Windows creates a .PIF file when it sets up an application for you, Windows automatically uses that .PIF file. If you have copied a .PIF file from an application directory to your Windows directory, you can tell Windows to use the .PIF file by choosing Properties in the File menu of the Program Manager. In the Command Line box, enter the drive, directory, and filename of the .PIF file, instead of the executable program file.

Keys to Success

The Program Manager is your first interface with Windows. To gain more control over this interface, you will want to set up your own program groups and program items.

To create a program group, choose New from the File menu in the Program Manager. Specify Program Group in the dialog box that appears; then enter a group name (description) and choose OK.

You can move or copy programs into the new group. First activate the new group window. To move a program item, drag the program icon from its current location to the new group window. To copy the program item, press the CTRL key while dragging the icon. To create a brand-new program item, choose New from the File menu. In the dialog box that appears, specify

Program Item; then enter the program item's name (description) and specify the file (command) Windows will execute to start the application.

To assist you with the process of setting up applications in group windows, you can use the Windows Setup program in the Main program group to have Windows scan your hard disk and create a list of all the applications stored there. Then you can determine if you want them added to group windows.

Windows can run non-Windows applications because it reads a program information file (.PIF) that indicates the necessary computer resources to reserve for an application. Most of the time Windows uses the default .PIF file (_DEFAULT.PIF), or a .PIF file that is included with the application. Sometimes a .PIF file is created by Windows when you set up the application and add it to a group window.

What Do They Mean By...?

Non-Windows Application   A program not specifically designed for Windows that can still be run under Windows. In order to have an icon for a non-Windows application, Windows must be able to read a .PIF file.

PIF Editor   A program for editing the entries in a .PIF file.

Program Group   An organized group of programs (applications). A program group can appear as an icon or a window.

Program Information File (.PIF)   A file that contains program information for a non-Windows application.

Program Item   An application program represented by a named icon that is accessible from a program group.

Windows Application   A program specifically designed to utilize the features of Windows.

Using the File Manager 8

The files that you create with your application programs represent a valuable investment of your time and knowledge. You will want to be certain to retain them safely and organize them efficiently for continued use. Windows includes a special application, the File Manager, that lets you easily manage your files, as well as organize them so you can quickly find the information you need.

Instead of having to switch to DOS for file management tasks, you can use the File Manager to

- Graphically view the directory contents of your disks

- List the files stored in your directories

- Copy, move, delete, and rename your files

Opening the File Manager

The information you work with along with your applications is stored in data files on your disk. The Program Manager shows you only the applications you have available, rather than all of the files you have created. This is where the File Manager comes in—it lets you see and work with the individual files you have stored on all your disks.

The File Manager is opened just like other applications. First, open the Main program group by double-clicking Main in the Program Manager; then double-click the File Manager icon (the file cabinet). You'll next see a window containing a diagram of the current directory on your hard disk, something like the following screen.

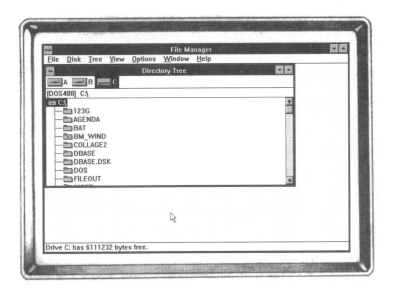

Closing the File Manager

Closing the File Manager window is like closing other Windows applications. You can double-click the File Manager's Control Menu box, or press ALT-F4. If you prefer to use a menu, open the File Manager's File menu and choose Exit. Exiting Windows also closes the File Manager.

When you exit the File Manager, you are prompted to confirm your request. Choose OK to leave the File Manager and return to the last active application. You also have the option of turning on or off the Save Settings check box; turning on Save Settings tells Windows to remember the menu settings for the next time you use the File Manager.

Opening and Closing the File Manager

To open the File Manager and look at the contents of a disk, activate the File Manager just like you do other applications. Double-click the Main group in the Program Manager, and then double-click the File Manager icon.

To close the File Manager, you can press ALT-F4, double-click the File Manager's Control Menu box, or choose Exit from the File menu.

The File Manager Window

The File Manager shows you a graphical representation of the contents of your disk. The initial window that is always present in the File Manager is the Directory Tree window.

The *directory tree* for a disk drive initially lists the directories contained in the drive's main (*root*) directory. Each of the windows in the File Manager is called a *directory window*. A directory window can contain either the directory tree or the file contents of a directory.

A disk is organized like a tree. The *root directory* is like a tree trunk from which the rest of the tree branches extend. Without branches, the leaves of the tree would have to grow directly from the trunk, limiting the tree's growth. The same is true for the root directory of a disk. Putting all of your files in the root directory makes it difficult to find the file you want, and you'll soon run out of room. So you'll want to split the root directory into branches.

The branches of any *parent directory* on a disk are called *subdirectories*. Just as a tree's branches might split into smaller branches, subdirectories can be parent directories in their own right, and split into additional levels of subdirectories. Each subdirectory can contain files as well as other sub-directories. The individual files are like the tree's leaves—most of your files will be stored at the lowest directory level, just as most of a tree's leaves are attached to the finest branches. Although files are usually at the tips of the directory structure, they are very important since they contain your data.

Note: In this book, as in most computer documentation, the word **sub-directory** *is frequently shortened to* **directory**.

The File Manager shows you visually how a particular disk drive (drive A, B, C, etc.) is organized into directories and files. Initially you see only the directory tree, with the first level of subdirectories shown directly under the root directory. No files appear in this list. When you need to, you can tell the File Manager that you want to see more detail. You can add the next level of subdirectories below the first level of parent directories, and you can open other directory windows to display the contents of a selected drive and directory. Each window is separate, so changing what appears in one directory window does not change the contents of other directory windows.

Changing the Drive Displayed in the File Manager

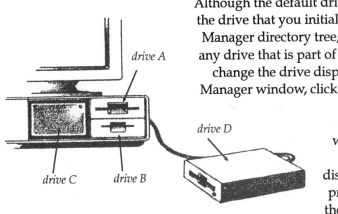

drive A

drive D

drive C   drive B

Although the default drive (usually C) is the drive that you initially see in the File Manager directory tree, you can look at any drive that is part of your system. To change the drive displayed in the File Manager window, click one of the drive icons at the top of the directory window. You can also change the displayed drive by pressing CTRL and the drive letter, for example, CTRL-A to change from the current drive to drive A. The File Manager uses various icons to represent floppy disk drives, hard drives, network drives, and virtual drives. In the illustration just below, notice the difference between the icons for floppy drives A and B, and hard drive C:

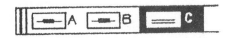

Working in the Directory Tree Window

The directories you first see in the Directory Tree window are only the first level of directories below the root directory. On some disks there will be several additional levels of subdirectories. The File Manager tells you graphically when a directory has subdirectories, and you can add these subdirectories to the tree display. A parent directory that has subdirectories is indicated by a + in its folder icon.

To expand the directory tree (display an additional level of subdirectories), just click the folder icon of the directory you want to expand. File Manager then adds the next level of directories to the tree, and changes the + in the folder icon to a –, as shown:

You can also expand a directory by pressing the UP ARROW or DOWN ARROW key to highlight the directory, and then press the + (plus) key.

When a folder icon contains a –, you can compress it and remove a level of directories by clicking the icon or highlighting it and pressing the – (minus) key.

Opening More Directory Windows

Once a directory tree shows the level of directories that you want to look at, you can open one or more directory windows that display the contents of specific directories. You can even open more than one directory window for the same directory. Opening additional directory windows lets you look at several directories at once. For example, you may want to compare the contents of two different directories to see which one has the latest version of a file.

To open another directory window, double-click the directory's name or icon in the directory tree that is already displayed. This displays another directory window containing the contents of the selected drive and directory. (You can also do this by pressing the UP ARROW or DOWN ARROW key to highlight the directory name, and then pressing ENTER.)

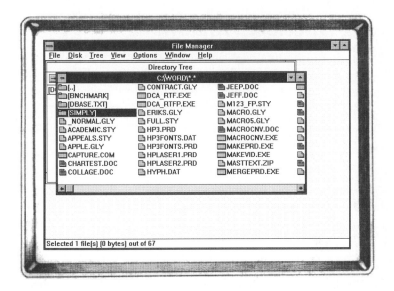

Once a directory window is opened to display a directory's contents, you can see all of that directory's subdirectories and files. You can use the keyboard arrow keys, or the mouse and the window's scroll bars, to change the part of the directory listing that appears within the directory window. You can also use the keyboard or mouse to select a file in the list and perform a necessary file management task, such as copying, moving, deleting, or renaming. (See the section, "Working with Files in Directory Windows," later in this chapter.)

When you want to switch to another directory window that is visible in the File Manager, just click it to activate it. Or you can choose the window name in the Window menu. Each of the directory windows has a name. The one containing the current directory tree is called the Directory Tree window, and the other open directory windows have displayed in their title bars the names of the drive, directories, and files that they contain. The directory windows are document windows that you can size and arrange, as you learned in Chapter 4, "Moving and Sizing Windows."

Closing Directory Windows

When you are finished using a directory window, you will want to close it to free up File Manager window space for the other directory windows you are using. To close a directory window, double-click the window's Control Menu box, or press ALT-HYPHEN to display the Control Menu box and choose Close. You can close every directory window except for the Directory Tree window.

Working with Files in Directory Windows

Notice in the previous illustration that Windows uses different icons for different file types. The file icon for program files (.EXE, for example) looks different from the icon of a Microsoft Word document (.DOC) file, or a data file that does not match a defined file type (.DAT or .GLY, for example). Program files have a rectangular icon; data files have one or another form of a square icon with a turned-down, upper-right corner.

Initially, a directory window only displays the icons and names of directories and files. You can expand this display to include additional information. You can list the size of each file; the time and date each file was last saved or each directory was created; and the attributes of each file. (*File attributes* are special characteristics that you or a program can assign to a file, such as indicating that a file is read-only so you cannot overwrite it.)

To display the expanded version of the file list, choose File Details from the File Manager's View menu. When you want to return to the more concise listing of just directory and filenames and icons, choose Name from the View menu. Here is an example of the beginning of an expanded directory window:

C:\WORD\SIMPLY*.*				
[..]		11/11/91	02:00:38 PM	——
OMH.STY	3584	04/29/91	03:28:16 PM	—— A
PIECE2A.DOC	19456	10/19/92	12:52:44 AM	—— A
SIMP2.DOC	18944	10/19/92	01:58:56 AM	—— A

Moving and Copying Files

 You can use the File Manager to organize your files so your information is logically stored on your hard disk, and other disk media as well. Organizing a disk is like sorting a hand of cards into suits; you want to put the files in locations where you will be able to find them.

To manage and organize your files, you need to be able to move and copy them to other locations (drives/directories). When you need to change the organization of files on your disk, you can use File Manager to move files from directory to directory. (You might have too many files in an existing directory, for example.) When you want to create a backup copy of a file, or a copy that you can use as a model for a new document, you can use File Manager to make those copies.

To move or copy a file, you simply drag the file from its existing location to a new location. Windows makes the following assumptions about your action:

If you drag a file to another directory on the same disk drive, Windows assumes that you want to move the file. If you drag a file to a location on another disk drive, Windows assumes that you want to make a copy of the file.

Using more specific keystroke instructions, as explained in a moment, you can also tell Windows that you do in fact want to move a file to another disk, or make another copy of a file on the same disk.

Thus, to move a file from one directory to another on the same disk, drag the file icon to its new location. For example, you can move a file to another directory by dragging its icon to the directory, or copy to a disk by dragging it to a disk icon. The new location to which you drag the file can be any visible directory window even if the directory window is minimized to an icon, a drive icon above the directory tree, or a directory name in the directory tree or a directory window.

When you do want to move a file to another disk, you'll need to be more specific in your instruction to Windows: you have to press the ALT key as you drag the icon to its new location.

When you do want to make another copy of a file on the same disk drive, you'll also need to be more specific: in this case, press the CTRL key as you drag the icon to its new location. For instance, you may need to make multiple copies of the same file in several directories on the same drive.

After you drag the file icon and release the mouse (and the ALT or CTRL key, if applicable), Windows displays a dialog box that asks you to confirm that you want to move or copy the file. By checking the message in the dialog box, you are able to confirm that Windows intends to move or copy the file, and thus make sure you have made the correct request. When you are certain of your actions, select Yes to confirm your request. Windows then moves or copies the file to the location you have chosen.

Moving and Copying Files

To copy or move a file, drag the file icon to a new directory icon, to an open directory window, or to a minimized directory window. If you need to move a file to another disk drive, you must also press the ALT key as you drag the file icon. If you need to copy a file to another directory on the same disk drive, you must also press the CTRL key as you drag the file icon.

Deleting a File

If you have created a file you no longer want, you can delete it to keep your disk from being cluttered with unwanted data. When you delete a file from a disk, it is no longer available. To make sure you don't regret your decision, it's a good idea to make a copy of the unwanted files to a floppy disk (as a backup in case you change your mind), and then delete the original on the hard disk.

To delete a file from File Manager, select the file to delete in the appropriate directory window. Then choose Delete in the File menu. (Notice in the File menu that you can also execute this option by pressing DEL.) Next, Windows displays a Delete dialog box that looks like this:

To delete the file, choose the Delete button.

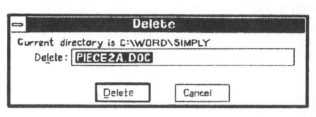

Before Windows processes the file deletion, it prompts you for confirmation of your request. You can choose Yes to delete the file or No if you change your mind. After the file is deleted, it no longer appears in the directory window.

Renaming a File

Ideally, you would never have to change a file's name; but circumstances are rarely ideal. You may need to change filenames so that files that contain similar data have similar names. Or perhaps you have made a spelling mistake that you want to correct. Whatever the situation, Windows lets you rename any file. Just select the filename in the appropriate directory window of the File Manager, and choose Rename in the File menu. Windows displays a dialog box that looks like this:

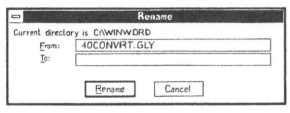

The From text box displays the current filename. In the To text box, type the new name that you want for the file. Once you have typed a new filename, select the Rename button to rename the file.

Caution: When you enter the new filename in the To box, be careful what you use as the three-character filename extension. Unless you are sure you want to use a different extension, you will usually want to type exactly the same extension that appears after the period in the original filename. The filename extension is used by many programs to define the format used for their data files. If you change the extension, you may not be able to use the file again.

Formatting a Disk

Yet another convenient use for File Manager is preparing unused disks to receive data. *Formatting* a disk is another task Windows can help you with so you do not have to return to DOS. Many of the most frequently used disk formatting options are available from a dialog box that makes their selection easy. Formatting a disk with the File Manager makes including formatting options such as selecting the disk capacity easier.

To format a floppy disk, select Disk on the File Manager menu and choose Format Diskette. If you have multiple disk drives, a dialog box appears so you can select the drive you want to use. (You'll select the drive letter from a Disk drop-down list box, and then choose OK.) Another dialog box then displays a warning about the potential loss of data during formatting. To proceed, choose the Format command button.

The next dialog box lets you choose the disk's capacity (if your drive can format high density disks) and whether the disk includes system files. For example, if you have a drive that can accommodate high-capacity disks, the last dialog box looks like this:

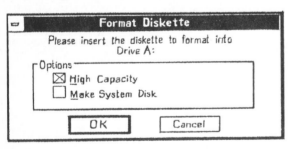

For a high-capacity drive, you can mark the High Capacity check box to format a disk to be 1.2MB or 1.44MB depending on the disk size. If you do not want to format in high capacity, make sure you select the High Capacity check box to unmark it. If your disk drive only formats to 360K or 720K, you will not have this check box.

To format a boot disk (a disk you can insert in the A drive and use to boot up your computer), mark the Make System Disk check box. This will cause the format process to add essential system files to the disk after formatting it. Be aware that a boot disk cannot store as much data as a regular formatted disk, because of the space consumed by the system files. To start the formatting process, select OK. After a disk is formatted, click Yes or No to indicate if you want to format another disk.

Keys to Success

The File Manager provides an interface to manage and organize your files that is easier to use than DOS. The File Manager provides a graphical display of the disk organization and of the contents of any directory on the disk. To start File Manager, open the Main group window and select File Manager.

File Manager contains at least one directory window called the Directory Tree window. You can change the disk drive that is displayed in the directory tree by clicking a drive icon above the directory tree, or by pressing CTRL and the letter of the drive. To open more directory windows in the File Manager window, double-click the directory icon in the directory tree, or highlight the directory name and press ENTER.

In the directory tree, folder icons represent directories; icons with a + indicate directories that contain subdirectories. You can add these directories to the directory tree by clicking the folder icon or highlighting it and pressing + (plus). Expanding a directory to display its subdirectories changes the + in the folder icon to a –. You can remove a level of directories from the display by clicking the parent directory name or by highlighting the parent directory and pressing – (minus).

You can use the File Manager to perform many file management tasks, such as copying, moving, deleting, and renaming files. Moving and copying files among drives and directories is accomplished by dragging the file icon from its current location (directory) to another. The File menu also contains Delete and Rename options for performing these file management tasks.

You can also use File Manager to format disks, with the Format Diskette option on the Disk menu.

What Do They Mean By...?

Boot Disk   A disk that contains system files so you can load the operating system by starting the computer with the disk in the disk drive.

Directory Tree   A diagram of a disk's directory structure that can be expanded or contracted to show more or fewer subdirectory levels.

Directory Window   A window in the File Manager that contains a directory tree or the contents of a directory on the disk.

Disk Capacity   The amount of data a disk can store depends on how the disk is made. 5 1/4-inch floppies usually can hold 360K or 1.2MB (high capacity) and 3 1/2-inch diskettes usually can hold 720K or 1.44MB (high capacity) of information. A hard disk may vary from 20MB to 120MB.

File Attribute   Information about a file that indicates settings, such as whether a file is read-only.

Formatting a Disk   Setting up a disk so you can store your files on it. If the disk has any information on it, that information will be removed when you format.

Parent Directory   A directory that contains subdirectories.

Root Directory   The initial and highest directory level that is present on every disk.

Subdirectory   A directory at a level lower than the parent directory.

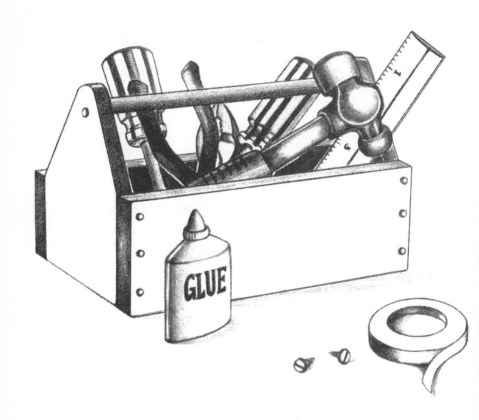

Customizing with the Control Panel

Part of feeling comfortable with your work environment is knowing you have control over it. To help you feel in control of the Windows environment, the Control Panel contains options that let you *customize* many aspects of Windows's behavior and appearance. The settings in the Control Panel affect every application that you run under Windows as well as Windows itself.

The Control Panel provides tools that make you an interior designer as you select colors and patterns for the desktop. Other Control Panel features make you a technician, as you set your computer's date and time and adjust the mouse's performance. You also get to be a manager over components such as the keyboard, communication ports, the printer, and the fonts it uses for your printed output. Once you learn even a few of the Control Panel options, you will see how your version of Windows can be personalized so it is different from anyone else's.

In this chapter you will learn how you can change the screen appearance, switch mouse buttons, set the date and time, change the installed printers, and add and remove fonts. The Control Panel has other options for changing other features about Windows but they offer more advanced options than you will want to learn about right now.

Working with the Control Panel

The Control Panel program in the Main program group puts you in charge of many of the Windows settings. You activate the Control Panel in the

same way you activated File Manager in Chapter 8, by double-clicking the Main group window, and then double-clicking the Control Panel icon. You'll then see a 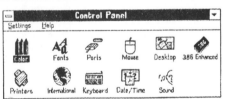 window containing an icon for each available type of customization, as shown here.

To open any of the Control Panel programs, double-click the icon. Each of these icons controls a different set of customizing options, as follows, and you will explore some of these in this chapter.

Icon	Customizing Functions
Color	Changes the color of various screen elements
Fonts	Adds or removes display and print fonts
Ports	Sets up your system for communication with other computers
Mouse	Customizes mouse operation, including swapping the left and right mouse buttons
Desktop	Lets you select wallpaper or patterns for the desktop
Sound	Enables/disables the warning beep
Printers	Installs printers and makes printer settings
International	Sets currency and other format options
Keyboard	Adjusts the repeat rate for the keyboard
Date/Time	Sets the date and time
386 Enhanced	Available only on 80386 computers to set resource sharing
Network	Available only on a networked system to control network connection

Using the Control Panel to Customize Windows

The Control Panel programs allow you to customize many aspects of your Windows environment. To use the Control Panel, open the Program Manager and follow these steps:

1. Double-click the Main program group.

2. Double-click the Control Panel icon.

3. Double-click the Control Panel icon that represents the type of change you want to make, or choose an option from the Settings menu.

Changing the Look of the Desktop

One way to personalize Windows
and the applications you use
with it is by changing the
color scheme of the desktop.
You can also add a flair to your
display by changing the pattern
of the desktop on which
windows are displayed.

Changing Display Colors

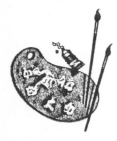

Color has an effect on your emotions. One day
you might be receptive to seeing your screens in
vibrant red and blue; on another day you might
prefer more subdued shades. On days when you
have been in front of your computer screen for
quite a few hours, you may find that giving your
eyes a new color scheme to look at makes it easier
to get through the rest of your workday. You can apply different colors to
your window display using the Control Panel's Color program.

To start Color, double-click its icon, or highlight the Color icon and press
ENTER.

Choosing a New Color Scheme

The Color dialog box allows you to select from many predefined display
color schemes, like the Windows default color scheme that you get when
you first install Windows. In these color schemes, the active and inactive
windows on the desktop will be in different colors. The screen element
colors are selected to contrast with text and menus, to make it easy to read
any part of the window. The colors and hues have been chosen to harmon-
ize with one another, and yet have a sufficient amount of contrast.

To look at the color scheme options, you can drop down the Color Schemes drop-down list box. As a reminder from Chapter 3, you can drop down the box by clicking the DOWN ARROW or by pressing ALT-DOWN ARROW. Use the DOWN ARROW key so the screen colors change to demonstrate each color scheme, and so you can see what you will get with each selection. You can use this view-and-choose method to pick the color scheme you like best, or choose one using the following list:

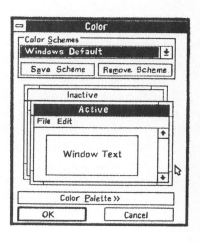

Color Scheme	Colors Used
Windows default	Royal blue, grey
Arizona	Gold, muted blue and green
Bordeaux	Purple, wine, mauve
Designer	Turquois, grey blue, wine
Fluorescent	Magenta, lime green
Monochrome	Grey tones
Ocean	Cool blues and greens
Patchwork	Eggshell, light green, turquoise
Rugby	Red, blue, light yellow
Pastel	Pale blue, green, yellow, pink
Wing tips	Grey, brown

Coloring Individual Screen Elements

If you do not want to be limited to the predefined color schemes, you can design your own. You can designate a specific screen element and then choose a color for it from a *color palette,* just as you would select a paint sample from a color chart.

To activate the color palette, choose the Color Palette command button. Next, click the diagram of the sample window elements above the Color Palette command button to select the screen element you want to change (it will appear in the Screen Element drop-down list box). As you select each screen element, Windows highlights a color box to indicate the color the screen element currently uses. You can paint the screen element a different color by clicking a different color box in the palette. The screen elements available for color changes include the active screen title bar, inactive screen title bar, window text, and inactive screen border. When you have the color scheme that you want to keep, select the Save Scheme button, type the name for the color scheme and select OK.

Changing Desktop Patterns

One of the things that you can change with Control Panel's Desktop is the desktop pattern. You can change from the subdued default pattern to an even simpler pattern, or something a lot flashier, like tulips or Scottish terriers. The pattern you choose covers the entire desktop.

Another desktop option you can select is a *wallpaper* pattern that covers the entire desktop with a repeating design. You can choose from options such as a chess board, party accessories, ribbons, and other novel designs. Wallpaper designs are stored in files with a .BMP filename extension. You can choose to put your wallpaper design in a tiled arrangement to cover the entire desktop, or just have a single copy of the wallpaper design in the center of the desktop. For example, you will want to select the Tile option when the wallpaper design is small, as in PYRAMID.BMP, and select the Center option for a large design such as CHESS.BMP.

If you choose both a pattern and wallpaper, you will only see the wallpaper, as it is applied to the desktop after any pattern. In the following example, the desktop pattern is set to Spinner.

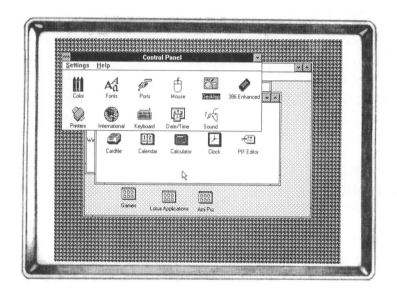

To change your desktop pattern:

1. Double-click the Desktop icon in the Control Panel, or choose Desktop from the Settings menu.

2. In the Desktop dialog box, select the desired pattern from the Name drop-down list box.

3. Click OK or press ENTER.

To change the wallpaper covering the desktop:

1. Double-click the Desktop icon in the Control Panel, or choose Desktop from the Settings menu.

2. In the Desktop dialog box, select the desired wallpaper from the File drop-down list box.

3. Select Tile to cover the desktop with the wallpaper, or select Center to place a single copy of the wallpaper design in the center of the desktop.

4. Click OK or press ENTER.

Customizing Your Mouse Operation

There are several features about your mouse that you can change. One thing you can control is which button, left or right, is the primary button used for finalizing mouse operations. If you are right-handed, you are probably satisfied with the default mouse arrangement, where the left button is the primary button. If you are left-handed, however, you might want to reverse the roles of the mouse buttons. This is called swapping the mouse buttons. Here's how to make this change:

1. Double-click the Mouse icon in the Control Panel, or choose Mouse from the Settings menu.

2. In the Mouse dialog box, mark the Swap Left/Right Buttons check box, which also switches the L and R.

3. Click OK or press ENTER.

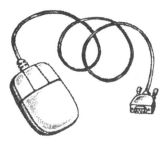

You can see in the dialog box that you can also change the timing for the interval between two clicks for them to count as a double-click, as well as the mouse tracking speed, which controls the relationship between the speed of the mouse device and the movement of the pointer on the screen.

Resetting the Date and Time

If your system has been turned off for an
extended period of time, or if your state
has just switched to or from daylight
savings time, the date or time in your system might not be correct. It is
important to keep these parameters accurate, since they are used for
various date and time identifiers in your Windows operation. For example,
every file that you create is given a date and time stamp so you can
determine the most recent version of the file (should you have more than
one copy of it).

To change the date and time setting, follow these steps:

1. Select Date/Time from the Control Panel, or choose Date/Time on
   the Settings menu.

2. In the Date & Time dialog box, click or tab to the element of the date
   or time that you want to change. (This is the day, month, or year of
   the date, or the hour, minutes, or seconds of the time.)

3. Type a new value for the chosen element. Or you can click the arrow
   buttons to increment or decrement the value.

4. Click OK or press ENTER.

Setting Up a Printer

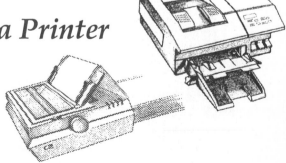

Windows manages
your initial printer
installation when you
first install the
program. If you decide

to add another printer or want to change the one that is installed, you will need to use Printers in the Control Panel. Printers helps you install printers, change how the printer is connected to your computer, establish printer settings, and select the printer that you will use most of the time when you print with a Windows application. The Printers options have no effect with non-Windows applications because these programs do not print through Windows.

Installing Another Printer

Before you can use a printer with Windows, Windows must know what printer you want to use. Adding a printer to Windows also adds a file called a *printer driver* to your hard disk. A printer driver file gives Windows and the Windows applications the information needed to print your data with the selected printer. Printers use their own printer drivers because most printers have their own unique commands and data structures.

To add a printer to use with Windows, follow these steps:

1. Double-click the Printers icon in the Control Panel window, or choose Printers from the Settings menu.

2. In the Printers dialog box, choose the Add Printer command button to expand the Printers dialog box as shown here:

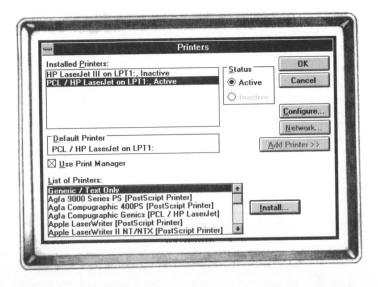

3. From the List of Printers list box, select the printer you want to add.

4. Choose the Install button.

Now Windows needs to copy a printer driver file from one of your Windows program disks to the hard disk. The next message you see prompts you for the disk containing the printer driver.

5. Put the disk containing the driver file into the disk drive, close the drive door, and click OK or press ENTER.

If the disk with the printer driver is not drive A, you must type the drive and the path before you select OK.

6. When you are returned to the Printers dialog box where you can see the printer you have just added in the list under Installed Printers, click OK or press ENTER to return to the Control Panel.

The printer you have just added is now included in the list of installed printers. You can make this printer the default printer, as described later in "Changing the Default Printer."

Selecting a Printer Port

A printer is connected to your computer through one of the various *ports*, or communications channels, in your computer. Ports have unique names such as LPT1 and COM1, where LPT represents a parallel port, and COM represents a serial port. Parallel transmission is faster because information is sent through the port on several simultaneous channels, rather than a single channel as is used for a serial port.

   If you change the connection between your computer and your printer, or if you add a printer, you may need to tell Windows how your computer is connected to the printer. To select a printer port for one of the installed printers, follow these steps:

1. From the Printers dialog box, select the name of the affected printer from the Installed Printers list box.

2. Choose the Configure button.

3. In the Printers-Configure dialog box, select the appropriate port from the Ports list box.

4. Click OK or press ENTER to return to the Printers dialog box.

Selecting Printer Settings

The Control Panel contains many of the important settings a printer uses, such as page size, and the *orientation* of printed data on the page (that is, whether it is positioned in landscape or portrait orientation). Each printer needs its own set of different printer options, so Windows changes the printer settings dialog box appropriately to match the features of your selected printer. To change a printer's settings, follow these steps:

1. In the Printers dialog box, select the name of the affected printer from the Installed Printers list box.

2. Choose the Configure button and then Setup.

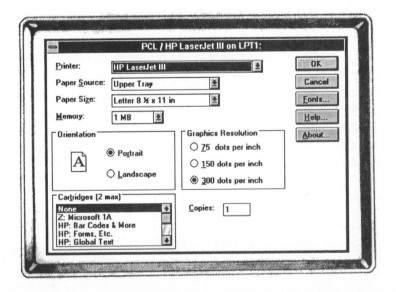

3. In the Settings dialog box that appears next, the name of the selected printer appears in the title bar. Change the printer settings as appropriate.

For instance, you may need to choose a different Orientation option, from Portrait to Landscape, for example, so you can print your information sideways on the page. You can also change the size of   the paper Windows thinks you will use to one of the predefined sizes. You still must change the paper in the printer, as well, to the new page size.

4. Choose OK twice to return to the Printers dialog box.

Changing the Default Printer

If you have several printers listed in the Installed Printers list box, one of them must be designated the *default printer*. "Default" means that Windows applications will use this printer unless you explicitly indicate that another one should be used. To designate one of the installed printers to be the default printer, follow these steps:

1. From the Printers dialog box, select the name of the new default printer from the Installed Printers list box.

2. Choose the Active option button in the Status box.

3. Click OK or press ENTER.

Note: Even after you designate a default printer, you can still change the printer a Windows application will use. Most Windows applications have a specific command that lets you change the printer you will use to print your data. See your application's documentation for instructions.

Choosing Fonts

A font is a collection of characters in a particular size and style used to display and print your data. All of the fonts that are available for your printer are installed in your computer's memory when you install your printer. Since all fonts take up some room in memory (and some require a lot), you will want to know how to remove and reinstall fonts.

Note: The one font that you should never remove is Helvetica, because Windows uses this font for much of the information it displays for you.

Removing a Font

When you need to remove a font to free up some memory for other tasks, follow these steps:

1. Double-click Fonts in the Control Panel window, or choose Fonts on the Settings menu to display the Fonts dialog box.

2. In the Installed Fonts list box select the font that you want to remove.

3. Choose the Remove button.

4. Click Yes or press ENTER to confirm that you want to remove the selected font.

5. Repeat Steps 2 and 3 for each font you want to remove.

6. Click OK or press ENTER.

Adding or Reinstalling a Font

When you again need a font that you have removed, you can reinstall it. The procedure is almost identical to removing a font.

1. Double-click Fonts in the Control Panel window, or choose Fonts from the Settings menu to display the Fonts dialog box.

2. Select Add.

3. Type the name of the font file that you want to add, and include the drive and directory if you are using Windows 3.0. You can use the Directories list box to change the font files with a .FON extension listed in the Font Files list box.

4. Click OK or press ENTER twice to add the font and leave the Fonts dialog box.

Keys to Success

Use the Control Panel program to change many of Windows's configuration options, to set up the Windows environment the way you want it. For example, you can

- Reset the date and time with Date/Time.

- Use Color to change display colors. If you want a more dramatic look, you can add wallpaper or an interesting pattern to the desktop, using Desktop.

- Mouse lets you alter the way the mouse works, including swapping the primary mouse button (left or right).

- With Printers you can install a printer to work with Windows and all your Windows applications. With the Fonts program you can install and remove printer fonts.

What Do They Mean By...?

Color Scheme   A set of colors that Windows uses for the different screen elements on the Windows desktop.

Control Panel   A program for customizing various aspects of the Windows environment.

Customizing   Changing Windows to better meet your needs.

Default Printer   The printer that a Windows program will use to print its information unless you direct the program to use another printer.

Font   A character style and size used for displaying and printing your data.

Ports   The connection between your computer and other equipment that lets you send information to other equipment such as printers or other computers. Computers use parallel or serial ports that tell the computer whether the communication line is a series of lines that can transmit information simultaneously or a single line to send information in a steady stream or a series of lines.

Printer Driver   A file that gives Windows the information it needs to work the printers your applications use.

Swapping Mouse Buttons   Making the right mouse button the primary button, or vice versa.

Using the Print 10 Manager

One of the most significant advantages of running application programs in Windows is being able to run more than one program at once, and switch between them. One task you'll do in all your programs as they run is send information to your printer. And when you do, of course you'll want the document from each application to print independently and without interference from any other application. You do not want the various programs that you have active sending output to the printer at the same time—it wouldn't do if you had budget information printed in the middle of payroll data. With Windows and its Print Manager running the show, you needn't worry about this kind of mix-up.

Windows handles this potential problem by letting each application send to Windows the data to be printed. Windows does the work of accepting the information from each application, and stores it in a *queue* or stack. Then Print Manager processes your requests for the material in the queue, one at a time. The Print Manager can organize all the printing you want to do. Most of the time the only evidence you'll see of the Print Manager at work is its icon at the bottom of the desktop. When you tell an application to print a document, Windows opens the Print Manager as an icon, prints the document, and then closes the Print Manager.

This chapter explains some of the features of Print Manager, and shows you how to start Print Manager, delete a job from the queue, interrupt a print job, and print without using the Print Manager.

Printing in Windows

When you take a document to a large print shop to be reproduced, many different departments within the print shop contribute to the production of your job. When you print a document in Windows, a similar combined effort occurs as the computer gathers information from several different sources. First you issue a print command in the application program, which tells Windows

Camera Dept.
Rm. 3112 ◄

Typesetting Dept.
Rm. 3113 ◄

Printing Dept.
Rm. 3114 ►

PRINT SHOP
Printing Dept.
3114

the data you want to print and how you want it printed. The information from your application can include instructions for printing each page with a boldfaced header, for example. To this information Windows adds the printer commands for your selected printer. For instance, if you have a word underlined in the document, the application tells Windows that the word should be underlined, and Windows adds the command that tells the printer to underline it. Each printer has different commands for print-ing with various fonts and attributes, and for printing graphics. Windows remembers each printer's commands so that your applications don't have to.

Windows combines the data to print and the necessary printer com-mands and places all this information in a temporary file. Then Print Manager can send the information from this temporary file to the printer when the job reaches the head of the print queue.

Windows does not require all of the resources of your system to handle a print job. Most of you have watched television while reading over the newspaper, and maybe even eating dinner at the same time; parts of your mind and body are involved in each activity. Windows does the same thing when it prints your documents. Windows allocates most of your computer's resources so you can work in various applications; this primary activity is said to run in the *foreground* in your computer. The remainder of your computer's resources are available for *background* activities.

Background activities have a lower priority than foreground activities, and this is a good environment for your printing jobs because printers generally operate much more slowly than your computer processor. Windows takes control of sending the information to the printer at a speed the printer can accommodate. And by doing this work in the background, plenty of computer power remains for applications in the foreground. You do not have to wait until your printer has finished printing to continue with your work.

Another feature of the Windows approach to print management is that each print request you make in an application program is stored in a temporary file; several print requests can be stored simultaneously. Once the application and Windows have put the information to print in a temporary file, the temporary file is added to the Print Manager's queue automatically. This print queue is nothing more than a list of the print jobs you have created; the jobs are listed in the order in which their temporary files are added to the queue. Once print jobs are sent to the Print Manager, you can view the queue, delete jobs, or make other changes.

Working with the Print Manager

When you take a print job to a print shop, your project is usually logged in and assigned a number, to insure that the job is not lost and is followed through to completion; Windows's Print Manager queue serves the same purpose. The Print 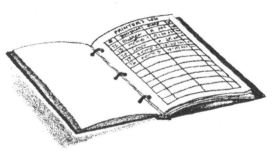 Manager can be opened for viewing, just like other application windows. In Print Manager's window you will see a list of the printing requests you have made.

Opening and Closing the Print Manager

Occasionally you will need to open the Print Manager and look at the jobs in the print queue. If jobs are currently waiting to be printed, the Print Manager icon will appear at the bottom of the desktop, where you can double-click it to get a closeup look at the queue. When there are no jobs in the queue, you'll need to activate Print Manager by double-clicking first the Main program group and then the Print Manager icon in that window.

To close the Print Manager, you can press ALT-F4, double-click the Control Menu box, or choose Exit from the Options menu.

To see if you currently have any print jobs in memory, look for the Print Manager icon at the bottom of the desktop. If it's there, you can double-click the icon to see the queue (described in the next section). If there are no jobs in the queue, you must access the Print Manager in the Main program

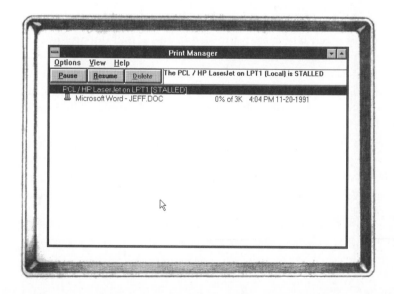

group. You're already familiar with this process—just open the Main group window by double-clicking Main in the Program Manager, and then double-click Print Manager. Your Print Manager window will appear.

Like other application windows, the Print Manager has a title bar and menu bar. Most of the time, you will not use the Print Manager menu since it controls printing automatically for you. The next line contains three buttons, Pause, Resume, and Delete, which you can use to temporarily postpone printing or cancel printing requests. After the three buttons there is information about whichever printer or print job is highlighted below. For printers, the Print Manager tells you the installed printer, where it is connected, and its status—such as STALLED, IDLE, or PRINTING. For print jobs, the Print Manager tells you where the print job came from, the time and date it was added to the queue, the size of its temporary file, and the percentage of the print job that is printed.

Looking at the List of Print Jobs

If you have a print job queued, as shown in the foregoing illustration, you will see the name given to the print job, the date and time it was added to the Print Manager queue, and the size of the file that Windows uses to store the information it will print. Because Windows adds printer commands to this file, it is often larger than the size of the actual document file being printed. The file size is measured in kilobytes (abbreviated as K), which approximates one thousand bytes. If you have more than one printer, the Print Manager separately lists the printer information for each installed printer with only the print jobs assigned to each printer listed under that printer's information.

As you request your Windows applications to print more documents, these print jobs are added to the bottom of the list. As Windows finishes printing a document, it removes that print job from the list and starts printing the next one. This continues until the printer has completed all your print requests.

Removing a Print Job

Ideally, when you tell Windows or a Windows application to print a document, everything that you print will look exactly as you want. But this is not always the case. You may start printing and then realize that you forgot to put a date in the header of a report, or change a paragraph on the last page of a three-page letter, or make some other change that means the document will need to be corrected and reprinted. Rather than wasting time and paper to finish printing the document, you can tell Print Manager to cancel the print output for that job.

To cancel a print job, activate the Print Manager window by clicking its icon at the bottom of the desktop. In the list of print jobs, click the one you want to delete, or use the keyboard arrow keys to move through the list and highlight the one to cancel. Next, click the Delete button, or press ALT-D. Windows prompts you to confirm that you really want to delete the print job. Select OK to remove the print job from the queue, or Cancel if you change your mind.

Note: Once the Print Manager has finished sending the print job, even if the printer hasn't finished printing, you cannot cancel the job from the list. You may be able to cancel the information stored in your printer by turning it off and on.

Removing a Job from the Print Queue

If you notice an error before a job finishes printing, you can delete the job, make the correction, and reprint it. To delete a job from the Print Manager queue, highlight the name of the job that you want to delete, and click the Delete command button or press ALT-D.

Pausing the Printing

When you tell a Windows application or
Windows to start printing, Windows starts
printing as soon as it has all the information it
needs to execute the task. Once a document
starts printing, you can temporarily interrupt
it. You might do this if your paper is not
loaded correctly, or you want to check
something in the document before all of it is printed.

To pause a print job, open the Print Manager window and select the print
job you want to suspend. Next, click the Pause button or press ALT-P. You
can also pause a printer, to interrupt all printing of documents sent to that
printer, by pressing one of your printer's buttons that has a label such as
On Line or Ready.

After you have suspended a print job, you can easily restart it. To tell
Print Manager to go ahead and resume sending information to the printer,
click the Resume button or press ALT-R.

Interrupting Printing

You can suspend printing of an individual print job or on a particular
printer, without canceling any print jobs. To temporarily halt printing, highlight the job that is currently printing, and click the Pause
button or press ALT-P.

Exiting the Print Manager

Exiting the Print Manager is like exiting other Windows applications. You
can double-click the Print Manager's Control Menu box, or press ALT-F4. If
you would prefer to use a menu, you can choose Exit from the Options
menu. If the Print Manager icon has been added to the desktop when you
request a Windows application to print a document, Windows will remove

the Print Manager icon and close the Print Manager for you when it finishes printing the last document. Exiting Windows also closes the Print Manager, but Windows will display a warning message if you still have print jobs in the Print Manager.

You can always leave the Print Manager open, but if your system does not have a lot of memory or you are using many applications, you will want to leave the Print Manager closed when it is not in use.

Printing Without the Print Manager

Although printing with the Print Manager offers significant advantages and helpful features, such as allowing you to queue print jobs from several applications simultaneously, you may occasionally want to print without using the Print Manager. For example, if you want to print out a report as quickly as possible, you will probably want to stop working in the foreground on other applications while Windows sends information to the printer in the background. In this situation you can bypass the Print Manager so your document gets printed more quickly.

To bypass the Print Manager, choose the Printers icon in the Windows Control Panel. This presents the Printers dialog box, containing settings for the printers you use in Windows. From this dialog box, unmark the Use Print Manager check box, and click OK or press ENTER. Then all subsequent printing you do in Windows applications with the same commands to print your data will not be done via the Print Manager. You'll need to wait until Windows and the application finish printing the document, and then you can continue working with other applications. This is just like printing with non-Windows applications, explained next.

Printing in Non-Windows Applications

Non-Windows applications do not recognize Print Manager's presence, but rather send documents directly to the printer. When you print in a non-Windows application, the application decides how to print the document and selects the specific printer commands needed to print the document. This is why you must select a printer when you install most non-Windows applications. You don't have to do this for most Windows applications because they use the printer you selected in Windows.

When you print with a non-Windows application, you must wait until the application completes printing before you can start printing another document or work with other applications.

Keys to Success

To utilize all the printing features that Windows provides, you will want to use the Print Manager for most of your printed output. Since this is the default arrangement when you request printed copies from any Windows application, the data to be printed and the printer commands needed are automatically written to a temporary file, which waits its turn in a print queue as a print job before being printed. The Print Manager is a program that manages the jobs in the queue.

You can delete jobs from the Print Manager queue if you change your mind about printing your document. You can also interrupt a print job while you correct a problem with your printer, and then resume printing.

If you want to print a job using all of the resources of your computer to finish as quickly as possible, you can print without the Print Manager. Non-Windows applications automatically use this approach; these applications do not allow you to create another printed document or use another application until a document has finished printing.

What Do They Mean By...?

Background Task   A task that does not receive top priority in your system operations. This task takes a back seat to foreground activities that normally receive more of your computer's resources.

Foreground Task   A task that receives high priority in the sharing of your computer's resources. Application programs normally run in the foreground while printing and similar functions occur in the background.

Print Job   A printing request added to the Print Manager queue.

Print Manager   A program supplied with Windows that manages all of the print requests from Windows applications. The Print Manager maintains a queue of all print jobs.

Queue   A list or stack. In the Print Manager, the queue contains the names of all the print jobs waiting for the printer's resources.

Windows Accessories for Recording Text

The Windows *accessories* are utility programs that come with your copy of Windows. You will probably find a use for many of the features the accessories provide.

Four of the accessories are designed to record and edit text in various forms. In Chapter 6 you were introduced to the important Clipboard accessory, which lets you temporarily store text that is already part of a document, and then move or copy the text to another location in the same application or a different one.

Here in Chapter 11 you will learn how to use the Write utility to create documents like memos or reports. You will also see how the Notepad lets you jot down ideas and messages while you are working on other tasks. And the Cardfile creates a set of electronic index cards on any topic. In this chapter, you will be introduced to the very basic features of these accessories to whet your appetite as you continue to discover all the tools Windows puts at your fingertips.

You can open any of the accessories during your work session in Windows. From any window, press CTRL-ESC and select Program Manager from the Task List. Then open the Accessories group from the Program Manager window, and double-click the icon for the accessory you want to use.

Using Windows Write

Double-click the Write icon in the Accessories group, and you'll see a blank Write workspace with a menu at the top. This window and its menu will look familiar to you if you've used another simple word processing package.

Write provides all the basic tools for text entry and editing, and it also allows you to apply some simple *formatting*, such as boldface and underlining. You can also change the page layout, which controls how data entered in Write appears on the printed page.

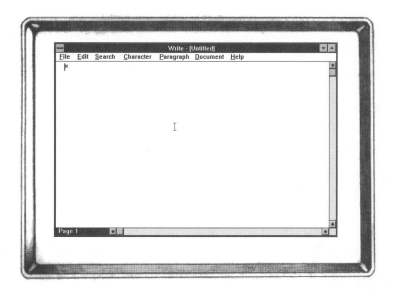

When you compare Write with some of the popular word processing packages available today, you'll find that Write doesn't include some of the more powerful features such as a spelling checker or thesaurus, or the ability to merge two documents such as an address list and a form letter. Although many people consider these features basic and indispensable to their word processing tasks, many others who have programs that offer these features rarely use them.

When to Use the Write Accessory

The Write accessory is a word processing utility. You can use it to create memos, reports, and letters.

Since Write comes at no additional cost when you buy Windows, and if you only occasionally need to create longer, more elaborate text documents, Write's simple text processing features may be perfectly adequate for your needs. Moreover, Write is always present in your Windows environment— you can use it when other software may not be conveniently available. Write is so easy to use that you may decide to use it for all your quick documents, even if you also have a full-scale word processing package.

Entering Text

To enter text in the Write window, all you need to do is type. Write uses *word wrap*; the text you type is automatically wrapped from one line to the next when an entire word does not fit at the end of a line. This feature means you can type continuously, without pressing ENTER to start new lines; just continue typing to the end of each paragraph, and press ENTER only at the end of the paragraph.

Remember: When entering text in Write, use the ENTER key only when you specifically want to end a line, such as the lines of an address block in a letter, or at the end of a paragraph. Also, press ENTER when you want to insert a blank line in your document.

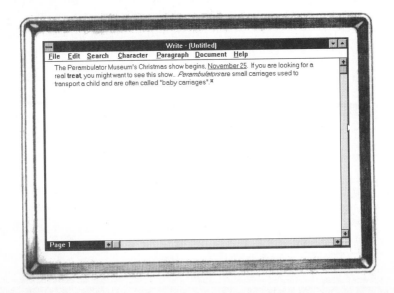

Word wrap makes a big difference when you edit your text; if you added and deleted words in a document where you had pressed ENTER at the end of each line, the lines in the document would no longer be full, and your right margin would take on a jagged appearance that might look something like this:

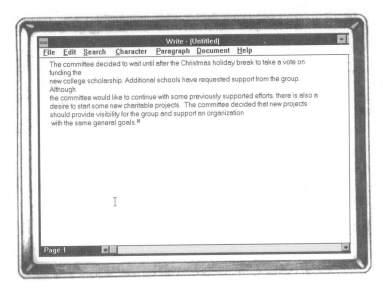

You can use the BACKSPACE key to delete the character to the left of the cursor. Repeatedly pressing this key removes additional text.

Write supports the addition of *character formatting* as you type your document. For instance, you can make the characters in your text appear in boldface or italic, or underlined, as shown here.

You can add character formatting by choosing the desired attibute from the Character menu. You can also use these shortcut keys to invoke the formatting:

CTRL-B	Adds boldface
CTRL-U	Adds underline
CTRL-I	Adds italic

One way to add character formatting is to use the menu or the shortcut key before you start typing the affected text. Or, if you forget to do this, you can always select the text after it's typed, and then add the formatting. Just follow the instructions later in this chapter, in "Selecting Text."

Locating Text

The easiest way to move around in a Write document is to use the mouse. Just click the text you want to edit and the insertion point will move to that location. You will notice that the mouse looks like an "I" when you are pointing to text.

Another way to move around (navigate) within your Write document is to use the UP, DOWN, LEFT, and RIGHT ARROW keys to move in those directions. When you need to locate text a little further away, try these key combinations to get there more quickly:

CTRL-RIGHT ARROW	Moves to the next word
CTRL-LEFT ARROW	Moves to the previous word
CTRL-END	Moves to the end of the document
CTRL-HOME	Moves to the beginning of the document

Another option for navigating in a longer document is to choose Go To Page from the Search menu or press F4. Then type the page number that you want to move to, and press ENTER. The insertion point is immediately placed at the top of the page that you selected.

You may not be sure where the text is that you want to find. But with a little help from you, Write can locate it for you. To look for any sequence of characters up to 255 characters in length, choose Find from the Search menu. Type the text that you want to look for in the Find What text box. You can also refine your search by marking either or both the Whole Word and Match Upper/Lowercase check boxes.

- Select Whole Word when you want Write to find your text only if it is an entire word. For example, with Whole Word marked, Write would not find *iron* in *ironing*.

- Select Match Upper/Lowercase when you want the match to occur only if both the characters and the capitalization match.

When you are finished specifying your search criteria, click the Find Next command button or press ENTER to initiate the search.

To look for additional occurrences of the search text, choose Find Next repeatedly as needed. Once it has found the last match, a message box indicates that the search operation is complete; you will need to select OK and then press ESC (or double-click the message box's Control Menu box) to proceed. If Write cannot find any occurrence of the text that you specified, it displays a message to that effect, and you will need to select OK to proceed.

Editing Your Documents

One of the most significant advantages of creating documents in a word processing program is that it is easy to modify and change your text. Write, too, helps you with these tasks. You can add words, sentences, and paragraphs. You can delete entire passages of unwanted text. Perhaps the most helpful text editing operation is moving and copying text to a new location.

Selecting Text

Once you select a group of characters in your document, you can perform an editing action on all the text that is selected. Although you can select text with the keyboard by holding the SHIFT key down and pressing the arrow keys, you will probably want to use your mouse to select text because it is the eaiest way.

To select text with the mouse, move the mouse pointer to the left of the text in the workspace; this area is called the *selection area* and, when moved into this area, the mouse changes to slant to the right. If you click the mouse once, you select the line that the mouse pointer is leaning toward. Double-click the mouse, and you select the paragraph containing that line. Press

CTRL while clicking the mouse, and you select the entire document. You can also select text by clicking one location and dragging the mouse to another point in your document.

Once a character or passage of text is selected, you can apply one of the format options described earlier in "Entering Text." For instance, by pressing CTRL-B you add boldfacing to the selected text. Or, if you want to delete the selected text, press DEL after making your selection. Selecting text is also the first step in a move/copy operation, discussed next.

Moving and Copying Text

Like other Windows applications that use the Clipboard to copy and move text, Write has an Edit menu with Cut, Copy, and Paste options. The Edit menu also has more advanced options for changing pictures that you have copied from the Clipboard. Here's how to move text to a new location:

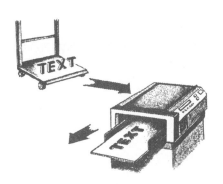

1. Select the text to be moved.

2. Choose Cut from the Edit menu.

3. Place the insertion point in the new location for the text (in the same Write document or in a document in another application window).

4. Choose Paste from the Edit menu.

Copying text is just as easy; follow these steps:

1. Select the text to be copied.

2. Choose Copy from the Edit menu.

3. Move the insertion point to where you want the copy of the text (in the same Write document, or in another application window).

4. Choose Paste from the Edit menu.

Repaginating Text

When you rearrange the text in a document, or add or delete text in a document, page breaks will usually not occur in their original locations. You may wind up with some pages that contain too little text, or too much. Write does not automatically repaginate your edited document, so you will want to request a pagination operation before printing, or you may not be happy with the final results.

To paginate a Write document, all you need to do is choose Repaginate from the File menu. If you want, you can tell Write to let you approve each page break; then click OK to begin checking the document.

Working with Document Files

You can save any Write document on a disk; just choose Save As from the File menu. Type a filename and click OK or press ENTER; Windows adds a .WRI filename extension for you. To use the saved file at a later time, choose Open from the File menu, highlight the desired filename, and press ENTER.

For subsequent changes you can choose Save from the File menu. You will not need to supply the filename. If you want to save a file under a new name, you can use Save As.

Changing the Layout

Write lets you change the appearance of printed text in several ways; a few are listed just below. (You will need to make these changes before requesting a printed copy.) These are just some of the basic features offered through Write's menus. You will see more features offered in the menus as you use them.

- If you do not want to use the default single line spacing, you can select either 1-1/2 or double-spacing. Choose the desired line spacing from the Paragraph menu.

- If you do not want to use the default left alignment that places text at the left edge of each line, you can choose either centered or right alignment from the Paragraph menu.

- You can change the margins, or the amount of white space that appears on any side of the printed text. Choose Page Layout from the Document menu, and then change the setting for the Left, Right, Top, or Bottom margin.

Printing

Printing your Write document is easy. All you need to do is select Print from the File menu. If you installed several printers with Windows, you may want to first choose Printer Setup from the File menu and specify the printer that you want to use.

Using Windows Notepad

The Notepad accessory is designed to work just like a paper notepad, and is always at hand to help with all your daily tasks. You can use Notepad to record short notes to yourself and others; to jot down a phone message for a co-worker, or items for your grocery list that you remember while working on next month's budget; or to maintain a to-do list for when you finish current tasks. Notepad creates text files without any special characters, such as the ones a word processor adds to designate formatting, and is a fine tool for creating short, uncomplicated documents.

You can also use the Notepad to keep a time-log file that records the date in front of your log entry each time that you open the Notepad. Use this to keep track of daily activities or phone calls.

When to Use the Notepad

Typically you will want to use Notepad just as you would use a paper notepad, to record messages to yourself and others, and notes about other projects that you might think of as you work on something else. The Notepad is ideal for creating shorter documents that don't need formatting. Notepad will also maintain a log file of date-stamped entries.

Recording a Note

To start recording a Notepad entry, you must first open Notepad by double-clicking its icon in the Accessories group. Once the Notepad is on the screen, all you need to do is start typing. The Notepad does not use the word wrap feature of Write; if you want text lines to automatically wrap to the next line, you'll need to choose Word Wrap from the Edit menu.

Recording a Time-Log File

You can use the Notepad for recording date-stamped messages in a special time-log file. Although you can always date-stamp a Notepad message by choosing Time/Date from the Edit menu or pressing F5, the Notepad lets you keep a file that adds an automatic entry of the current date every time you open  the Notepad. To do this, you need to type **.LOG** (capital letters are required) on the first line of the Notepad workspace.

The first few entries on a Notepad used in this fashion might look like this:

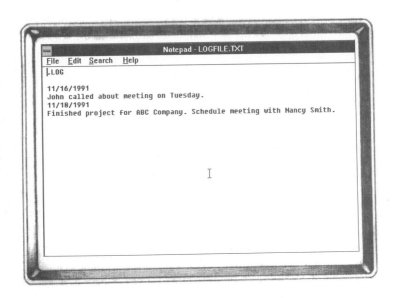

When you use the log file, you will want to save the log file as you add messages. If you are adding notes to it constantly, you will want to keep the log file open, possibly as an icon. By the way, you can have more than one version of an accessory open at once. This means you can have one Notepad window open containing your log file and another Notepad window open containing your current project's notes.

Using Write Features in the Notepad

Some of the features you learned to use with Write will also work in the Notepad. These include the text navigation keys, the text searching techniques, and the text selection methods. The same commands you learned for the Write accessory to save and open your files also apply in Notepad. Windows adds a .TXT filename extension to Notepad files to distinguish them from Write and other word processing files. Try out the options you learned for Write to see what will work in the Notepad.

Using Windows Cardfile

At one time or another you have probably used a set of index cards. You may have recorded notes for a term paper, recorded addresses  and phone numbers, created a small database of supplier names, or recorded each of the CDs in your music collection. You used the cards to help you organize that recorded information, so it was easily accessible. You can use Windows Cardfile for the same.

The Cardfile accessory is nothing more than a set of electronic index cards. You can record any type of information that you want on these cards, and access it again quickly, in several ways. To see the Cardfile accessory on your screen with a blank card, double-click the Cardfile icon in the Accessories group.

There are two areas on every card that you complete. The *index line* is where you enter the text that will be sorted to keep the cards in sequence. You can think of these index lines as the entries that you might find in the index of a book; in both cases, the purpose of the index item is to make it easy to find the data that you want, quickly. The other, larger area of the card is where you record the information you want to file.

When to Use the Cardfile

The Cardfile accessory is a set of electronic index cards. You can use it to record client names and addresses, phone numbers or messages, music records or CDs in your collection, or facts for a term paper.

Adding a Card

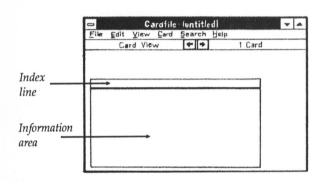

Index line

Information area

When you first open the Cardfile, you will see a blank card on the screen. The insertion point is positioned to begin typing text in the information area of the card, but you will want to add an index entry first. This is the entry the Cardfile uses to create a sorted list of all the cards that you create in a particular set of cards (a *cardfile*). Let's use this opening blank window to create a new index card.

1. In a blank card window, choose Index from the Edit menu or press F6. In the dialog box that appears, type the index line entry in text box, and click OK or press ENTER.

2. To add the card's main information, just start typing. This information might be a client's name, address, and phone number, for example.

3. When you are ready to add another new card, you can choose Add from the Card menu or press F7. The new blank card is added to the top of the stack.

4. In the dialog box that appears, type the index line entry in the Add text box, and then click OK.

5. Again, a new card appears and you can complete the information text.

As you keep adding cards, the new one is always added at the top of the stack. Once you have added cards, you can change them. Editing the information area is just like editing in the Notepad. To change the index line, press F6 and edit the information in the text box before you select OK. You can also edit the index line by double-clicking it.

Moving to Another Card

Here's how to move among a stack of cards in a cardfile:

- Click the card you want to select.

- Click the arrows in the status bar (the line just below the menu bar) to move through the cards one at a time.

- Move to any card by using the PAGE UP and PAGE DOWN keys to move up and down scrolling from one card to the next.

- Use CTRL-HOME to bring the first card in the file to the front, and CTRL-END to bring the last card in the file to the front.

- To move a specific card to the front, choose GoTo from the Search menu or press F4, type part of the index entry for the card that you want in the GoTo Text box, and select OK.

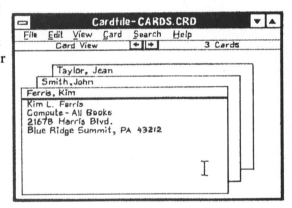

Deleting a Card

To delete a card, the card must be at the front of the stack. Choose Delete from the Card menu, and click OK or press the LEFT ARROW and ENTER to confirm that you want to delete the card.

Finding a Specific Card

You can search the information text in your stack of cards to find a specific card. Cardfile begins your search with the card containing the insertion point, and searches forward. To begin the search, choose Find from the

Search menu. In the dialog box, type the text you are looking for in the Find text box, and click OK. You can repeatedly choose Find Next from the Search menu or press F3 to look for other occurrences of the search text, until you find exactly the card you want or until Cardfile displays a message that there are no more matches.

Creating a List of Index Entries

Using Cardfile's *list view*, you can see a list of the cards in a cardfile, based on the index line entries from all the cards, in alphabetical order. To do this, choose List from the View menu. Use the UP and DOWN ARROW to move through the list. To switch back to the individual card view, choose Card from the View menu.

Printing Cards

You can print one card or the entire stack. If you want to print just the top card, choose Print from the File menu. To print all the cards, choose Print All from the File menu.

Saving the Cardfile

You can have many different sets of cards (cardfiles). Before creating a new cardfile you must first save the one you are working on. To do this, choose Save from the File menu. In the dialog box, type a name for the cardfile that will assist you in finding it later; then choose OK or press ENTER. To open an existing cardfile for later use, choose Open from the File menu.

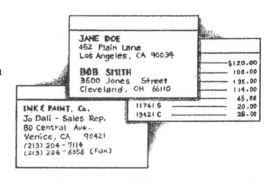

Keys to Success

Windows provides a variety of accessories that are available at all times during your Windows sessions. To start one of these accessories, press CTRL-ESC and select Program Manager from the Task List; open the Accessories group from the Program Manager window; then select the icon for the accessory that you want to use.

- The Write accessory is a word processing program. You can use Write to create reports, memos, and any other type of document that includes basic formatting.

- The Notepad accessory is for shorter, unformatted documents. You might think of Notepad when you want to record a few phone messages while working on another project. You can also set up Notepad to function as a time-log file, by embedding a .LOG statement at the beginning of the Notepad file.

- The Cardfile is like a stack of electronic index cards. You can write anything you want on these cards, and enter an index line for sequencing the cards.

What Do They Mean By...?

Accessory   A program included in Windows that provides computerized versions of many items you have on a desktop, including a notepad and index cards.

Cardfile   A Windows accessory that imitates a set of index cards to store many types of information.

Formatting   An addition of an appearance attribute to enhance the displayed and printed text in a word processing document. Formatting options available in Write include boldface, italic, and underlining.

Index Line   A line on each card in a cardfile that can be used for indexing all the cards in the stack.

Layout   In word processing, this refers to the arrangement of the printed page. For example, line spacing and margins (white space) are important elements of layout.

Repaginate   To go through an edited document from the beginning and decide where each new page of text should begin. Write has a feature that you can use to do this.

Selecting Text   Marking text—one character or a long passage—so that you can invoke one command that will apply its result to the entire selection.

Selection Area   The left edge of a Write document that you can click to select an entire line or paragraph of text.

Time-log File   A file that includes the date, which you can add text to.

Word wrap   A feature used in word processing programs; it automatically wraps to the next line any word that does not fit completely at the end of the current line.

12
Additional Windows Accessories

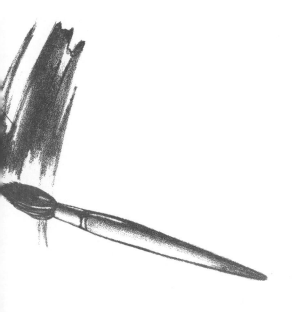

Windows has additional accessories other than the ones you have looked at thus far in this book. There is a Clock that you can display on the screen whenever you want to know what time it is. You can use the Calendar accessory to keep track of all of your appointments. The Calculator lets you perform simple arithmetic computations, or even scientific calculations. Paintbrush lets you create drawings with lines, shapes, text, and color. And with the Terminal accessory (and a modem) you can send and receive data over a phone line to and from another computer. This chapter only provides a simple introduction to these accessories. You can then decide which ones you want to learn more about.

As you learned in Chapter 11, you can open any of the accessories during your Windows work sessions. From any window, press CTRL-ESC and select Program Manager from the Task List. Then open the Accessories group from the Program Manager window, and double-click the icon for the accessory you want to use.

Using the Calculator

The Windows Calculator lets you do on screen all the computations you normally do with a pencil and paper. And since Windows lets you switch between applications with ease, you can start the Calculator to perform a quick computation while you are working with a word processing or financial application. The Calculator has a Standard version and a Scientific version.

$$\sqrt[3]{8}$$

$$\begin{array}{r} 21,597 \\ +\ 36,244 \\ \hline 57,841 \end{array}$$

$$12 - 4.3 = 7.7$$

$$\begin{array}{r} 185 \\ 25\ \overline{)\ 4625} \\ \underline{25} \\ 212 \\ \underline{200} \\ 125 \\ \underline{125} \\ 0 \end{array}$$

To start the Calculator, double-click its icon in the Accessories group. A calculator window like this appears:

When you are finished using the Calculator, double-click the Calculator's Control Menu box or press ALT-F4. (This accessory does not have an Exit menu option.)

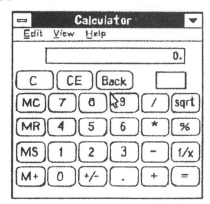

Entering a Computation

The buttons on your Windows electronic calculator can perform all the tasks of a hand-held model. With your mouse, you can point to any button and click it to enter the number or symbol on the selected button. Or you may find it just as easy to type the numbers and symbols on the keyboard. For example, to compute the cost of ordering 8 items at $2.50 each, plus $1.75 in postage, follow these steps with the Calculator on your screen:

1. Click or type **8**.

2. Click or type * (the symbol for multiplication).

3. Type **2.50**.

4. Click or type +.

5. Type **1.75**.

6. Press ENTER, which is the same as =, to end the computation. The calculator displays the result, 21.75.

7. Press ESC to clear the result from the calculator display.

Using the Scientific Calculator

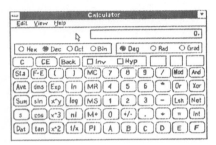

The Scientific Calculator lets you work with different number systems—that is, number systems that use a base other than the base ten used by the decimal number system. This version of the Calculator also performs some statistical functions.

To switch to the Scientific Calculator, choose Scientific from the View menu of the Calculator window. You can work with the numbers and

---

The Calculator Buttons

The two Windows calculators, Standard and Scientific, have many buttons that work just like their equivalents on your hand-held calculator. Here is a review of the Calculator's buttons and their actions:

C	Clears the current calculation
CE	Clears the current entry
BACK	Backspaces
MC	Clears the value in memory
MR	Displays the value in memory
MS	Stores the displayed value in memory
M+	Adds the displayed value to memory
sqrt	Calculates the square root of the displayed number
%	Calculates a percentage
1/x	Calculates the reciprocal of the displayed number (1 divided by that number)
+/−	Changes a positive number to a negative number and vice versa

On the Scientific Calculator you will find additional buttons that allow you to run more complex calculations.

symbols of this calculator just as you did with the standard model. To switch back to the default calculator again, choose Standard from the View menu.

Using the Calendar

The Calendar accessory lets you record your daily appointments in detail, and also lets you look at an entire month's appointments. Start Calendar as usual, by double-clicking its icon in the Accessory group. The initial view displayed is for the current day, with time interval entries that look like this:

You can begin recording appointments right away, or you can look at a different view of the Calendar (explained in the next section). You can create multiple calendars, and use the File menu to name, save, and open them. This lets you create separate calendars for your business and personal life; or if you are sharing your computer with others, each of you can have your own calendar. Saving a calendar is a familiar process—as with other files in other accessories, you save a calendar by choosing Save in the File menu and giving the calendar a name; and you retrieve a calendar by selecting it from the list that appears when you choose Open in the File menu.

When you are finished with your Calendar, choose Exit in the File menu. You will be prompted to save your calendar when you exit.

Changing the View of Time

When you first start the Calendar accessory, a daily calendar with one-hour time intervals is displayed. If you want to change the time interval used, choose Day Settings from the Options menu; for Interval, select the 15, 30, or 60 option button. You can also make the starting hour for your day's appointments a little earlier or later (the default is 7:00 A.M.); just type a new time in the Starting Time text box.

You can also change the calendar view to a month instead of a day. To make this adjustment, choose Month from the View menu or press F9. To return to viewing an entire day, choose Day from the View menu or press F8.

```
Calendar - (untitled)
File  Edit  View  Show  Alarm  Options  Help

1:35 PM  [←][→]   Monday, November 18, 1991
                    November  1991
     S    M    T    W    T    F    S
                              1    2
     3    4    5    6    7    8    9
    10   11   12   13   14   15   16
    17  >18<  19   20   21   22   23
    24   25   26   27   28   29   30
```

Recording Appointments

You can use the arrow keys to move between appointment times or click the desired time with the mouse. Once you have the insertion point at the desired time, you can type up to 80 characters of text to record information about the appointment.

You can also make notes on the scratch pad at the bottom of the Calendar window. Move the insertion point into the scratch pad area by clicking it or pressing TAB, and then type up to three lines of text. This scratch pad text is attached to the current date and is displayed when the date is viewed in either day or month mode.

Setting an Alarm

In Calendar you can set an *alarm* to remind yourself of appointments. The alarm can warn you of the approach of one or many appointments. If the Calendar utility is active, you will be reminded of your appointment with a beep and a dialog box. If the Calendar is minimized to an icon, the icon will flash and the computer will beep when the alarm time arrives. If the Calendar window is open but not active, the computer will beep and the title bar of the Calendar window will flash.

Here is a sample of an alarm dialog box displaying the text that was designated to display along with the alarm:

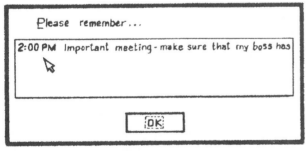

To turn off the alarm, you can click OK if the dialog box is displayed. If it is not, you will have to open the Calendar accessory before you can click OK in the dialog box.

Looking at a Different Day

To display a different day, you can choose Next or Previous from the Show menu to advance or move back one day. You can also choose Date from the Show menu or press F4, type into the dialog box a specific date you

want to see, and click OK. A third option is to click the arrow buttons that
appear between the time and date at the top of the calendar. (Clicking the
left-arrow button displays the previous day; clicking the right-arrow button displays the next day.) You can also use these arrows to shift forward
or backward one month in the Calendar's month view.

Displaying the Clock

Analog   *Digital*

The Clock is the simplest of all the accessories—its sole function is to
display the current system time. The default clock display is *analog*, in
which the time is shown on a traditional round clock dial with three hands.
The *digital* display option expresses the time in numbers, rather than clock
hands. You can change to either display by choosing Digital or Analog from
the Settings menu.

   If you want to remove the clock from the display, double-click the Clock's
Control Menu box or press ALT-F4. (This accessory, like Calculator, does not
have an Exit menu option.)

Using Paintbrush

Paintbrush provides all the materials that you will need to create your own
drawings. The Paintbrush Toolbox makes it possible to draw lines, curves,

boxes, circles, ellipses, and polygons. You can fill these shapes with a color or pattern, and add text and lines as needed to enhance the drawing. The Paintbrush window includes a Palette and a Linesize box to provide these additional options. Once you start Paintbrush by double-clicking its icon, you're ready to unleash all your creativity.

The cursor in the drawing window shows you where the part of the drawing you are working on (or the text you are typing) will start. You can use the mouse to move the cursor or you can use the keyboard. Depending on the changes you are making to the drawing, the pointer will have a variety of shapes.

When you have finished using Paintbrush to create your drawing, save it by choosing Save in the File menu, typing a filename, and clicking OK. Paintbrush adds a .BMP or .PCX filename extension. You can then retrieve your art for later use by selecting it from the list displayed when you choose

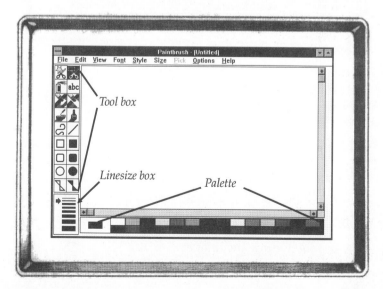

Open in the File menu. You can also use the Paintbrush to create and import graphics that you can then use with the Clipboard to put in other documents.

To exit the Paintbrush accessory, choose Exit in the File menu, or double-click the Paintbrush window's Control Menu box, or press ALT-F4.

Creating a Drawing

You can use any of the Paintbrush *tools* to create your drawing. These tools are represented by icons at the left of the Paintbrush window. Here are the basic steps for painting:

1. Select colors for the foreground and background, by pointing in the Palette to the color you want and clicking the mouse. For foreground colors (used to draw the elements of the image), press the left mouse button. For the background color, press the right mouse button.

2. Click a drawing tool.

3. Use the tool to draw the image.

The Paintbrush Drawing Tools

To select a drawing tool, click its icon. Here is a list of the icons and their functions:

Picks an irregular area of the graphic to change with Edit menu options

Picks a rectangular area of the graphic to change with Edit menu options

Paints a circular area filled with dots

Adds text

Changes an area's foreground color to the background color

Erases anything in the selected area

Fills an area until it runs into boundaries, such as other objects in the drawing

Paints color where you drag the mouse

Paints an arc between two points you designate, in the direction you select next

Draws a straight line

Draws a rectangle or square

Draws a rectangle or square filled with the foreground color, with a border in the background color

Draws a rectangle or square with rounded corners

Draws a rectangle or square with rounded corners filled with the foreground color, with a border in the background color

Draws a circle or ellipse

Draws a circle or ellipse filled with the foreground color and with a border in the background color

Draws a shape with a variable number of sides by letting you pick each corner of the object's shape

Draws a shape with a variable number of sides by letting you pick each corner of the object's shape, filled with the foreground color and with a border in the background color

Using Zoom

One of Paintbrush's handiest features is the zoom capability. Using Zoom In and Zoom Out on the View menu, you can magnify a section of your drawing to get a closeup look, or reduce it down so you can see the entire drawing.

Tip: Another way to increase the displayed area of your drawing is to use the View menu and temporarily remove the Toolbox, Linesize box, and/or the Palette from the window.

Printing in Paintbrush

When you have finished with your drawing and you want to print it, use the Print command in the File menu. You can select OK to print your entire drawing. Like printing with the other accessories, you can change which installed printer you will print to by choosing Printer Setup in the File menu and then selecting an installed printer and OK.

Using the Paintbrush

Now that you have learned the very basics of the Paintbrush accessory, you can try using it on your own. The drawing tools that Paintbrush offers are best used by spending some extra time with Paintbrush and trying each of the tools to see the results they produce. Once you have spent time playing with the different tools, you will be prepared to use them when you need to accomplish something. To try more of the Paintbrush features, you can copy drawings to the Clipboard and then paste them into other applications such as Write. You have already learned about the Clipboard so you already know how to use many of the commands in the Edit menu. To copy only part of a drawing to the Clipboard, select the area you want to copy with the Pick or Scissors tool first.

Using Terminal

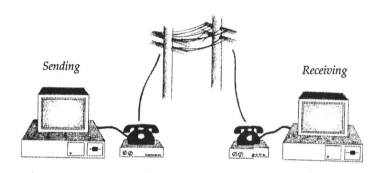

Sending

Receiving

If you have a modem, and a serial port or connector on your computer, you can connect with other computers in remote locations through the telephone lines. A *modem* takes information from your computer and sends it over the phone line, and takes information coming in over the phone line and sends it to your computer. The Terminal accessory provides the software needed to make this connection possible.

The most difficult part of using Terminal is setting the parameters needed to correspond with the settings of the remote computer system. To find out what settings are needed, first start Terminal by double-clicking its icon in the Accessories group. Then open the Settings menu and look at the parameters for the Communications, Modem Commands, and Terminal Preferences options. Once you set up these parameters to match the remote location, you're ready to send and receive.

Here are the basic steps to send a file to another computer:

1. Choose Dial from the Phone menu.

2. In the Dial text box in the Phone Number dialog box, type the number to dial

if it is not already set up for you. When you click OK or press ENTER, your computer uses the modem to dial this number. Once you are connected to the other computer's modem, you can start sending data.

3. From the Transfer menu, choose Send Text File or Send Binary File, depending on the format of the file to be sent. A text file is like the files you create with the Notepad that only use standard characters that you would find on a typewriter. A binary file includes additional characters such as the ones a word processor adds to indicate how the text should appear.

4. Choose Hangup from the Phone menu.

5. Choose Save As from the File menu, and specify a filename under which to save the current group of settings, so you won't have to reset them the next time you need to connect with the same remote computer.

6. Choose Exit from the File menu.

Keys to Success

Several of the Windows accessories provide alternatives to other, separate programs. These accessories provide a wide range of features that you might otherwise have to acquire by purchasing other software packages. The accessories and features you learned about in this chapter include the following:

- When you need to perform a computation, you can do it quickly and accurately with the Calculator accessory. The accessory is as easy to use as a hand-held calculator, but offers both a standard and scientific version, as well as the convenience of being part of Windows.

- The Calendar program lets you record all of your appointments in one easy-to-access location. You can even set an alarm so you don't miss a meeting.

- The Clock displays the current time in your system. You can choose an analog or digital display.

- The Paintbrush accessory lets you draw, color, modify, and save graphic images. You have a full complement of drawing utensils, colors, and special effects.

- The Terminal accessory makes it possible for your computer to interact with another computer, using modems and a phone line. Once a link is established, you can transfer data files between computers.

What Do They Mean By...?

Analog   A clock display that shows a clockface and clock hands to display the time in hours, minutes, and seconds.

Binary File   A file that is in a format understandable only to the computer. If you display the contents of this file, you will see unrecognizable, nonkeyboard characters.

Digital   A numeric indication of the time in hours, minutes, and seconds.

Modem   Short for Modulator/Demodulator. A device attached to a computer that lets it communicate with another computer by phone.

Paintbrush Tools   Tools that let you make different types of changes to your drawing.

Scientific Calculator   A calculator that provides additional calculation for advanced mathematical and scientific calculations.

Text File   A file that contains only text characters, as represented on your keyboard keys.

Zoom   To change the size of the displayed portion of a Paintbrush drawing. You can zoom in for a closer look at a small area, or zoom out for an overall perspective of the drawing.

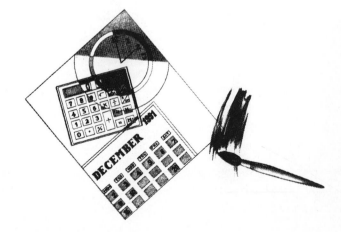

A
Installing Windows

Before you can use Windows, you must install it on your system. This installation process copies the Windows program files from the disks that come with the Windows package to your hard disk, and configures Windows for your particular hardware setup. Windows has a Setup program that guides you through the installation process. After you install Windows, you are ready to install your printers, and the Windows applications you want to use. Many applications specifically designed for Windows can be installed only after Windows is installed.

Starting the Windows Setup Program

To start the Windows Setup program,

1. Put Disk 1 in the drive (typically drive A) and close the disk drive door.

2. Type **A:** (or, if you are not using drive A, type the appropriate drive letter followed by a colon) and press ENTER.

3. Type **SETUP** and press ENTER. The Windows Setup program starts and displays a welcome message screen; press ENTER to proceed.

Setup first needs to know where on your hard disk you want Windows installed. The default location is C:\WINDOWS, but you can select another location by editing the C:\WINDOWS prompt to indicate the path (drive and directory) where you want Windows installed. Press ENTER to confirm your selection.

Setup next checks the path you have designated, to see that it has at least 6.3MB of disk space, the minimum required by Windows. If you do not have enough memory, Windows displays a message telling you to exit the Setup program by pressing F3. You can then delete files to make room on the drive where you want Windows installed, or select another location by pressing ENTER and specifying another path on a disk that has more than 6.3MB of available space.

Setup now checks your computer's hardware configuration and determines facts such as the DOS manufacturer, the display type, and the type of mouse attached to your system. This information is displayed on the screen. If any of the information is incorrect, press the UP ARROW to highlight the incorrect item. Press ENTER, and use the UP and DOWN ARROW to select the correct setting, and press ENTER again. When all of the settings are correct, press the DOWN ARROW until "The above list matches my computer" is highlighted, and press ENTER.

Now Setup starts copying files to your hard disk. You will be prompted to insert disks as necessary. When you see the prompt for another disk, replace the disk as instructed and press ENTER. After Setup copies some of the files, it changes to a graphical user interface that provides support for a mouse, at which point you can use your mouse to continue with the installation. Press ENTER or click Continue to proceed. The boxes with Xs in them indicate that you will set up the printers that you will use in Windows, set up applications on the hard disk to use in Windows, and read Windows's online README.TXT documentation (explained in the sections that follow).

Now Setup will copy more files to your disk—this time showing Setup's progress with each disk and the filenames that are copied. As before, you are prompted to change disks. When you see the prompt, make sure to put the correct disk in the drive and close the drive door. After this group of files is copied, Setup will establish program groups for the applications included with Windows, including the ones you will work with later in groups named Main and Accessories.

The next step for Setup is to prompt you about changing the CONFIG.SYS and AUTOEXEC.BAT files. These system files are used when you start your computer; they provide information such as instructions to DOS on where to look for files, and to load programs such as the one that operates your mouse. Windows adds commands to CONFIG.SYS that use your computer's memory better, and changes AUTOEXEC.BAT to put the directory containing Windows in the PATH statement. Unless you know you want to enter these commands yourself, press ENTER to have Setup do it for you. If you know you do not want these commands entered to the system files, press the DOWN ARROW twice and ENTER once; this prevents changes to your original system files and puts modified files called CONFIG.WIN and AUTOEXEC.WIN in the Windows directory.

Setting Up Printers for Windows

Once Setup has handled the changes to your AUTOEXEC.BAT and CON-FIG.SYS files, it presents the Printers dialog box. This dialog box lets you select the printers you will use with Windows applications, as follows:

1. Choose a printer from the List of Printers. To do this, use the UP and DOWN ARROW keys or click the scroll bar to change the section of the list of printers displayed; then click or highlight the printer you want to install. (To move faster within the list, you can move to the first printer that starts with a particular letter by typing that letter key.)

2. Once a printer is selected, click Install or press ALT-I. You may be prompted to insert another disk; if so, just switch the disk as usual, and click OK or press ENTER.

3. If you want to install more than one printer, press ALT-L or click the List of Printers, select another printer from the list, and click Install or press ALT-I.

Windows assigns the first printer you select to port LPT1, which means the computer sends information to that printer using the first parallel communications port. If you install more than one printer, the additional printers will have their port set to None. You can change a printer's assigned port by highlighting the printer in the Installed Printers list and pressing ALT-C or clicking Configure. From the Printers-Configure dialog box, select the computer port the printer is connected to and press ENTER or click OK.

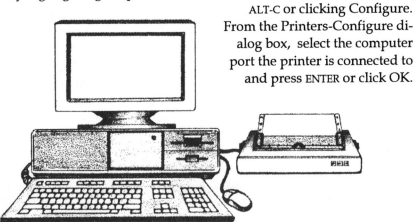

Now you need to determine which printer is the default printer (the printer Windows will use when you do not explicitly select another one). If the printer you want to use as the default is specified as "Inactive" in the Installed Printers list, highlight the printer in the list and press ALT-S for Status; then press the UP ARROW or click Active. Finally, press ENTER or click OK to process your Printers dialog box settings.

Setting Up Applications

Another part of Windows Setup installs applications within Windows so you can run them by selecting an icon on the screen. You'll do this in the Set Up Applications dialog box (after you install your printers).

First press ENTER to search all of the drives for applications to set up, or press the UP or DOWN ARROW to select a specific path to search for applications; then press ENTER. Windows searches the drive(s) and presents a dialog box that includes a list of the applications it has found. You can add all of these to Windows by clicking Add All or pressing ALT-D. To add applications one by one, move to an application in the list and click it or press the SPACEBAR. Like other list boxes, you can use the arrow keys and the scroll bar to move through the list. When all the applications you want to add are selected, click Add or press ALT-A.

You can also remove applications from the list; press TAB until the list box on the right contains the dotted selection box, move to the application you want to remove, click it or press the SPACEBAR, and select Remove or press ALT-R.

When you are satisfied with the list of applications to be added, click OK or press TAB until the OK button is outlined, and press ENTER. Windows adds these applications.

Notice how Setup divides the applications you add into two groups—those that are designed to run under Windows (Windows applications) and those not designed to run under Windows and that often run straight from a DOS prompt (non-Windows applications).

Viewing the Online Documentation

Windows includes a README.TXT file that contains additional information about Windows that is not in the Windows documentation manuals. This includes information about specific software or hardware you may want to use with Windows. After the applications are set up, Setup opens the Windows Notepad accessory so that you can use text files.

The Notepad is opened with the README.TXT file loaded. You can browse through it by pressing keys like UP ARROW, DOWN ARROW, PGUP, and PGDN, or by clicking the scroll bars. When you are finished looking at the file, click the File option and choose Exit from the menu that appears, or press ALT and type F and X. This takes you out of the Notepad, and completes the Setup program.

At this point, you can restart (reboot) your computer, start Windows, or return to DOS. If you made changes to your CONFIG.SYS and AUTOEXEC.BAT files, you will want to reboot your computer so the changes you made will take effect. If you want to immediately start using Windows, you can choose Restart Windows. If you want to return to the DOS prompt, choose Return to DOS. To choose one of these options, just click it, or press ALT and the underlined letter.

You have now completed the Windows installation process.

Changing Printers After Installing Windows

Once Windows is installed, you may subsequently need to add printers or change their settings. This is done with the same Printers dialog box that you use when you initially install your printers, as explained earlier in "Setting Up Printers for Windows." To access this box in order to change printers after installation, you need to use the Printers option in the Windows Control Panel. Here's how:

1. From the Windows Program Manager, open the Main group window.

2. Double-click the Control Panel icon.

3. When the Control Panel window opens, double-click Printers.

4. Windows displays an abbreviated version of the Printers dialog box you saw during installation, without the bottom half that includes the list of printers. At this point, you can add other printers or make changes to existing ones (as explained in the next two sections).

5. Click the OK button or press ENTER to save the changes you have made and return to the Control Panel.

6. Close Control Panel by pressing ALT-F4 or double-clicking the Control Menu box, which is the small box containing a hyphen-shaped icon in the upper-left corner of the Control Panel.

Adding or Changing Printers

Before you can use a printer with Windows applications, it must be installed for use with Windows. To add a printer to Windows, select the Add Printer button in the Printers dialog box. This expands the Printers dialog box to show the List of Printers you can install, and an Install button. Just like adding printers when you first install Windows, click or highlight a printer in the list. Then click Install or press ALT-I. You may be prompted to insert a disk; just put it in the drive as usual and then click OK or press ENTER. Continue adding all desired printers. Then you can make other changes to the printers you have installed.

To change how one of the printers is connected to the computer, highlight the printer in the Installed Printers list, and press ALT-C or click Configure. From the Printers-Configure dialog box, select one of the Ports options and press ENTER or click OK.

Changing the Default Printer

Another common printer change you may need to make is to change which installed printer you want to use as a default. Windows applications use the default printer unless you specify another one when you print your data. For the default printer, choose the printer that you want most of your Windows applications to use. To do this, highlight the printer you want to assign as the default in the Installed Printers list box; click Active for Status, or press ALT-S and then UP ARROW. This makes the selected printer the active one (the default), and all other printers inactive.

Index

Simply PCs
by Bob Albrecht

First-time computer users won't want to miss this beautifully illustrated guide that thoroughly explains what a computer system is and how to use it. This user-friendly book provides you with a clear overview of software applications, hardware devices, peripherals, and operating environments. You'll learn basic terminology and all you need to know to operate your computer effectively.

$14.95, ISBN: 0-07-881741-2, 197 pp., 5 3/4 X 8 3/4

Simply DOS
by Kris Jamsa

Here's the ideal DOS book for anyone who needs to learn the basics. DOS expert Kris Jamsa makes learning DOS simple, short, and painless. Clear, step-by-step instructions introduce the essential DOS commands that you need for everyday tasks. Covers all versions of DOS through DOS 5.

$14.95p, ISBN: 0-07-881715-3, 208 pp., 5 3/4 X 8 3/4

Simply Windows
by Mary Campbell

What is Windows and how can you use it? *Simply Windows* tells you all you need to know to get started with Microsoft's graphical user interface for IBM and compatible PCs. This simple introduction gives you the basics so you'll feel comfortable with Windows while getting fast results.

$14.95p, ISBN: 0-07-881743-9, 208 pp., 5 3/4 X 8 3/4

Simply 1-2-3
by Mary Campbell

Lotus 1-2-3 beginners will welcome this quick guide to the basics of the world's most widely used spreadsheet. You won't be baffled by spreadsheet programs when you finish this book. With many illustrations and computer screen displays, you'll quickly learn the fundamentals of setting up and using a 1-2-3 worksheet.

$14.95p, ISBN: 0-07-881751-X, 214 pp., 5 3/4 X 8 3/4